This book belongs to

"" *Every accomplishment starts with the decision to try.*"
John F. Kennedy

HOW TO USE THIS BOOK

Welcome to our recovery activity book!

We know that the recovery path can be tough, but we're here for you every step of the way. Each page is filled with activities carefully crafted to help you improve:

- Handwriting and tracing
- Memory skills
- Fine motor skills
- Cognitive functions
- Visual perception
- Language abilities

With practice every day, you'll see great progress. Every day is a new chance to move forward, and if you miss a day, it's okay, just start again when you can.

If one activity seems hard, it's okay to move on and come back to it later. Sometimes you'll feel more ready to tackle it! The exercises are not organized by themes so that it's more dynamic, allowing you to exercise your mind more.

Not sure if your answers are right? No worries! **You can find the solutions at the end of the book.** But, many activities have lots of right answers, especially the coloring and drawing ones. So, just do them the way you like!

We believe in your ability to recover, and we're excited to support you every step of the way.

Let's start this journey together!

TRACE THE SHAPES

Carefully trace the shapes, then color
if you'd like

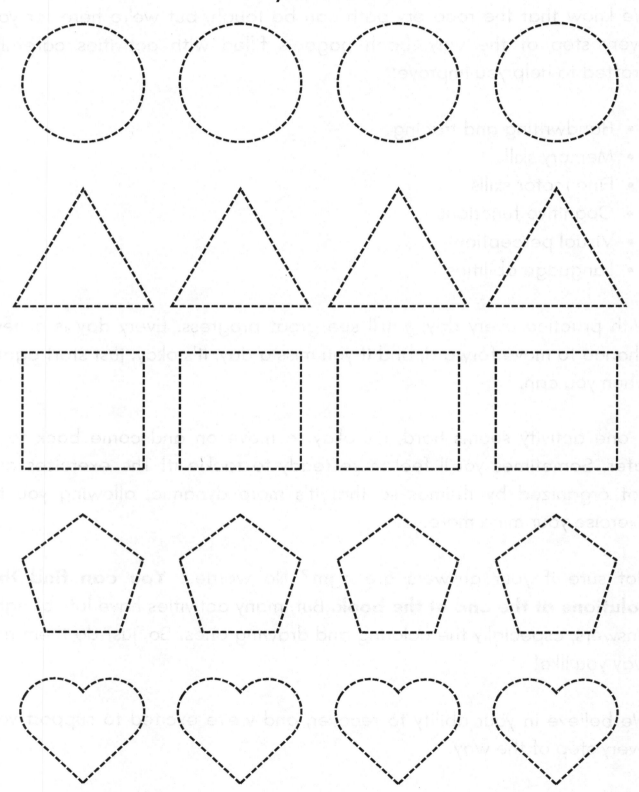

COMPLETE THE PATTERN

Draw the shape that comes next in the
pattern

Solution on page 196

COMPLETE THE LINES

Continue the following lines

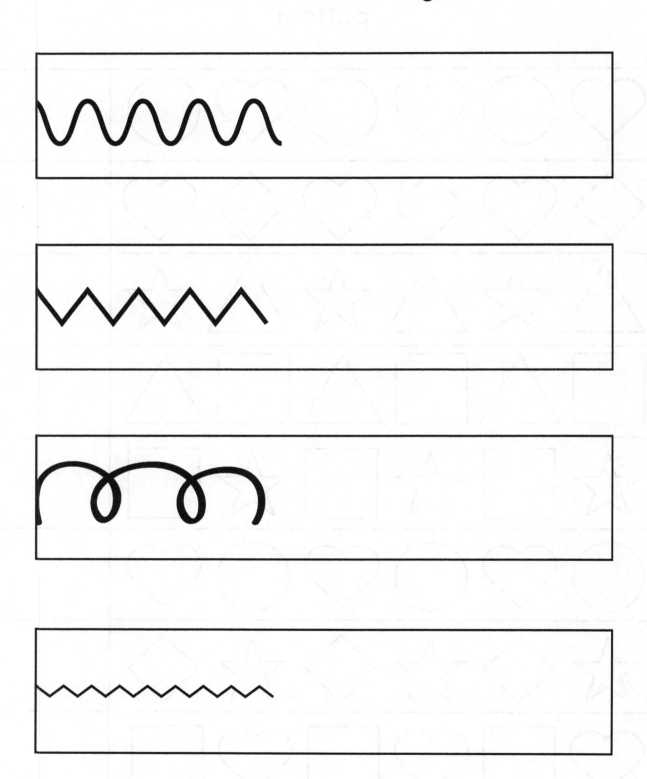

SHAPES CHALLENGE

Color 🎨　　　Trace　　　Draw ✏️

FINISH THE PICTURE

Draw the other halves and color the
pictures. Then, trace the words

Popsicle

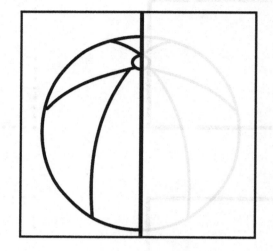

Beach ball

Seashell

Starfish

FIND AND TRACE

Find and trace the numbers 1, 3, and 5

Solution on page 197

PRACTICE HANDWRITING

Trace the word, then write it next to it

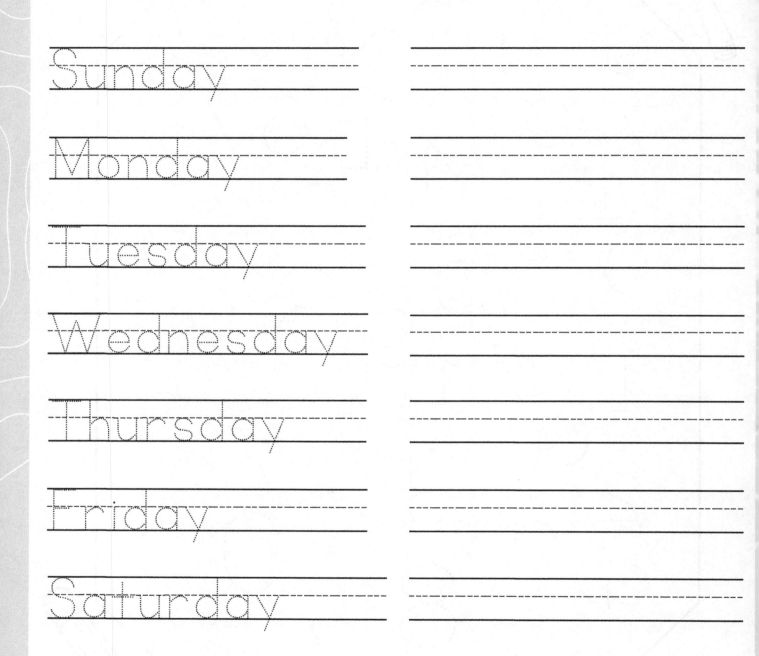

Sunday

Monday

Tuesday

Wednesday

Thursday

Friday

Saturday

TRACE AND COLOR

Trace the shapes, then color your own

We left this page blank so as not to interfere with the previous exercise.

If you don't do the exercise, feel free to use this page to draw or write whatever you like!

WHICH IS WHICH?

Connect the correct word to the matching image

Cap ●

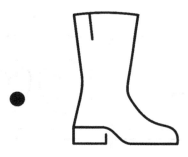

●

Boots ●

●

Sunglasses ●

●

Socks ●

●

Gloves ●

●

Solution on page 198

COUNT AND COLOR

Color the fruit based on the given numbers

4	
6	
5	
9	
8	
6	
3	

RECREATE THE PATTERN

Observe the patterns below, recreate them in the next box

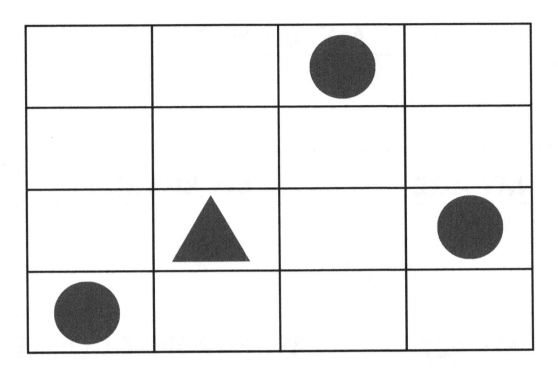

Your turn!

ALL ABOUT YOU

It's time to talk about you! Write down the information detailed below

MY NAME IS...

MY AGE

MY BIRTHDAY

MY PET

MY FAVORITE COLOR

MY FAVORITE FOOD

ONE THING I LIKE

COUNT THE OBJECTS - WINTER

Count how many objects there are of
each and write them down

Solution on page 199

COPY THE PATTERN

Observe the patterns on the left, draw
the same pattern on the opposite box

WHAT COMES NEXT?

Look at the sequence and identify which patterned block goes in the fourth spot, then mark it

1   2

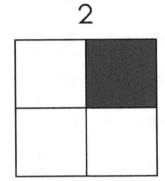

3

?

A   B   C   D

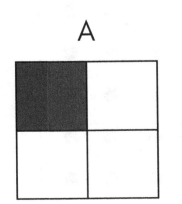 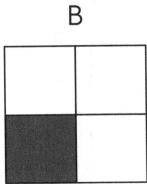 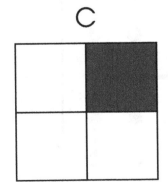 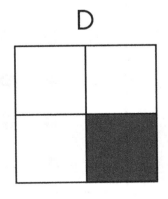

Solution on page 200

LINE THE DOTS

Trace a line by connecting the dots
following the pattern on the left

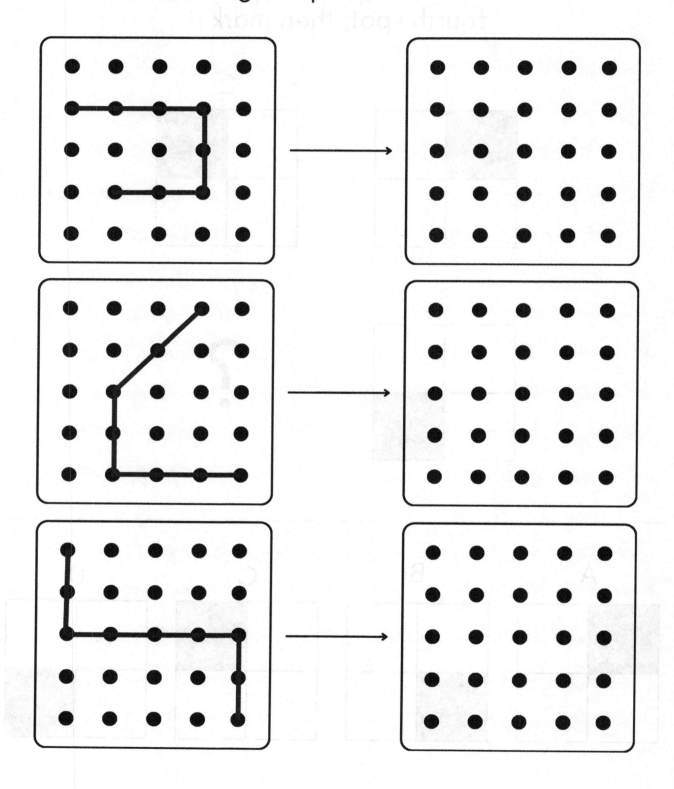

WORD SEARCH - NUMBERS

Find the items listed below

```
R  S  G  T  W  E  L  V  E  I  T  A
B  H  E  E  M  I  O  K  P  V  A  S
D  X  E  V  A  S  I  X  O  O  L  D
E  O  H  L  E  T  C  C  E  N  A  T
L  T  N  C  O  N  E  I  T  E  D  H
E  I  I  C  T  W  E  M  O  T  K  R
V  R  N  S  E  A  F  I  V  E  S  E
E  C  E  H  N  V  A  A  V  G  F  E
N  U  W  V  E  C  F  E  C  R  L  A
B  O  T  W  O  L  K  O  O  T  U  M
B  V  T  E  P  L  C  H  U  E  P  N
E  E  I  G  H  T  I  R  E  R  F  R
```

ONE	FOUR	SEVEN	TEN
TWO	FIVE	EIGHT	ELEVEN
THREE	SIX	NINE	TWELVE

Solution on page 201

MISSING VOWELS

Complete the following words with the correct vowels.

 p_g

 d_g

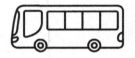 b_s

 b_d

 m_p

 b_g

 f_x

 b_g

 l_g

 r_t

Solution on page 202

SCISSOR SKILLS

Color in the rectangles and cut along
the lines

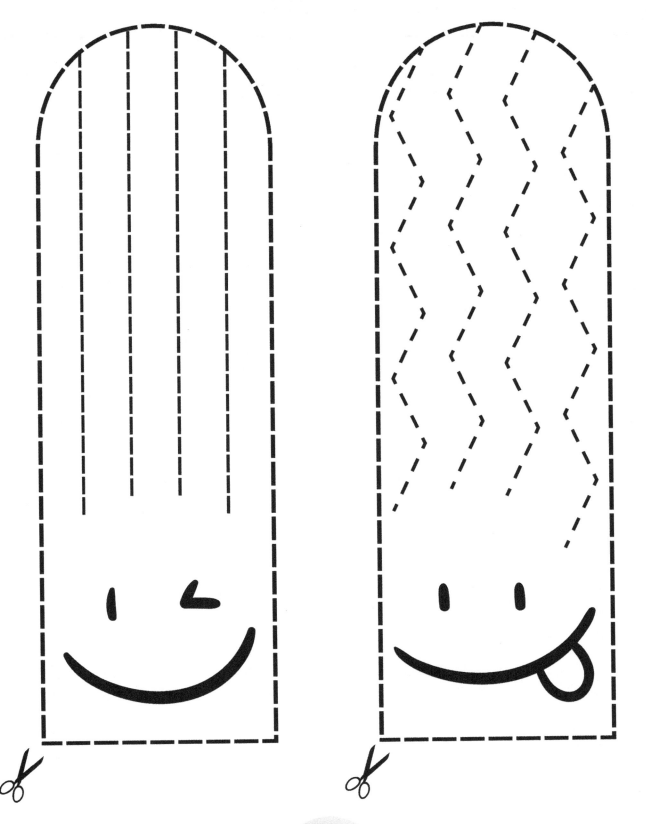

We left this page blank so as not to interfere with the previous exercise.

If you don't do the exercise, feel free to use this page to draw or write whatever you like!

COUNT THE OBJECTS - SPRING

Count how many objects there are of
each and write them down

Solution on page 203

UNSCRAMBLE

Unscramble the letters to find the words

BREA

_____

ROHIN

_____

FORG

_____

SANKE

_____

GIRLLOA

_____

EPHLENTA

_____

CMAEL

_____

CHTEEAH

_____

TCAUNO

_____

EGELA

_____

FAMLIONG

_____

CORDLIEOC

_____

Solution on page 204

PUZZLE PIECES

Read the names on the puzzle pieces
and draw the corresponding number

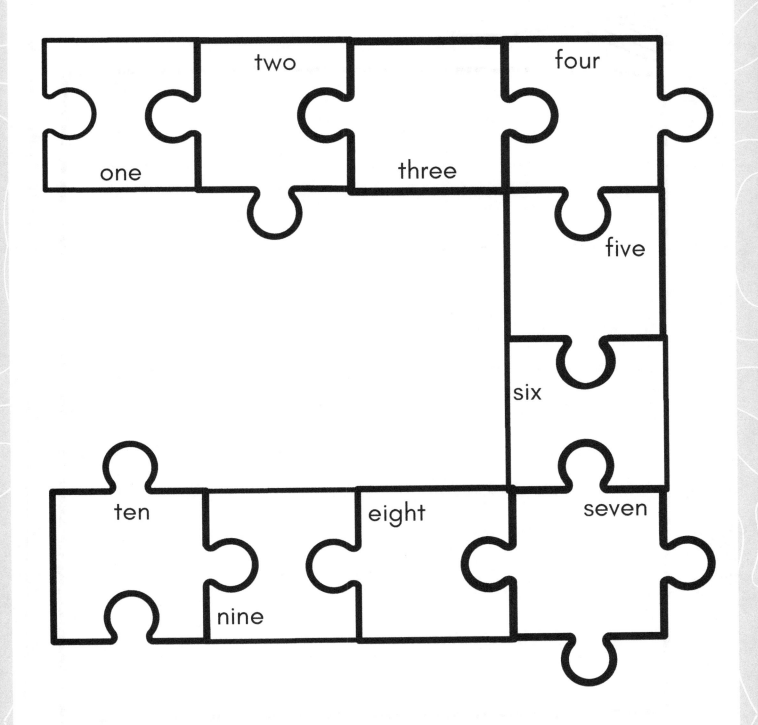

TIME TO WRITE!

Write yourself a short motivational message

EMOJI CHALLENGE

Copy each hand emoji with your hands

CROSSWORD NUMBERS

Complete the crossword puzzle by filling in the blanks with the name of each number

Solution on page 205

We left this page blank so as not to interfere with the previous exercise.

If you don't do the exercise, feel free to use this page to draw or write whatever you like!

MISSING LETTERS

Complete the following words with the missing letters

B   C   F   G   H

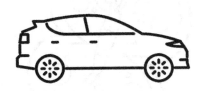

_ar

_at

_an

_ut

_ly

_um

_en

_ut

_at

_ot

_as

_oy

Solution on page 206

UNSCRAMBLE

Unscramble the letters to find the
words, then color the images

SORLFEW

RBID

BTUTEYRFL

_____

LUADYBG

ETRE

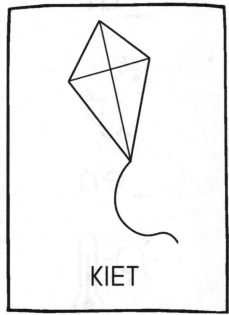

KIET

_____

Solution on page 207

THOUGHT EXERCISE

Read the following sentences and
write down whatever comes to mind

Health and Wellness

Think of 5 activities that help you relax:

1 _____

2 _____

3 _____

4 _____

5 _____

Think of 4 healthy foods you consume:

1 _____

2 _____

3 _____

4 _____

Think of 3 things you do to take better care of yourself:

1 _____

2 _____

3 _____

RECOGNIZE THE NUMBER

Read and respond to the following exercises to recognize the number 4

Make a 4 with your fingers

Trace the 4 with your finger

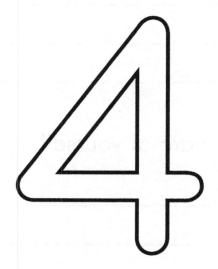

How many arms do windmills have? Count them

BUBBLE ADDITION

Add up these numbers and find the answer in the bubbles

$4 + 4 =$ _____ $4 + 3 =$ _____

$3 + 3 =$ _____ $4 + 5 =$ _____

$2 + 2 =$ _____ $1 + 2 =$ _____

$5 + 5 =$ _____ $2 + 3 =$ _____

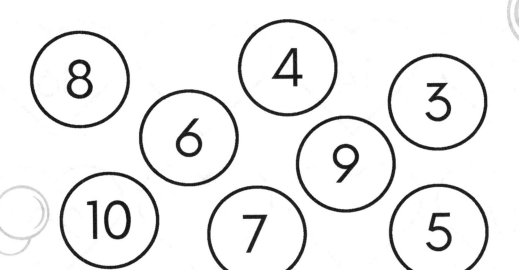

Solution on page 208

MISSING NUMBERS

Fill each heart with the missing numbers from 1 to 20

Solution on page 209

FRACTION EXERCISE

Circle the appropriate fraction from
the provided options

$\dfrac{1}{2}$ $\qquad$ $\dfrac{2}{3}$ $\qquad$ $\dfrac{3}{4}$

$\dfrac{1}{3}$ $\qquad$ $\dfrac{2}{4}$ $\qquad$ $\dfrac{1}{4}$

$\dfrac{1}{3}$ $\qquad$ $\dfrac{3}{5}$ $\qquad$ $\dfrac{1}{2}$

$\dfrac{2}{3}$ $\qquad$ $\dfrac{1}{5}$ $\qquad$ $\dfrac{1}{2}$

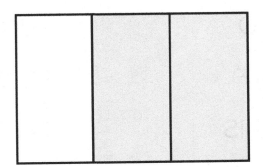

Solution on page 210

WORD SEARCH - SPORTS

Find the items listed below

```
V  S  O  B  A  S  E  B  A  L  L  Q
G  O  L  F  A  D  U  A  C  O  A  S
S  O  L  U  M  D  G  S  B  T  S  W
C  Y  C  L  I  N  G  K  O  E  N  I
B  S  O  M  E  E  Y  E  L  N  E  M
H  O  C  K  E  Y  N  T  U  N  T  M
H  C  S  E  N  Y  B  B  N  I  B  I
U  C  T  E  N  D  I  A  A  S  O  N
T  E  J  N  O  S  T  L  L  O  A  G
F  R  U  G  B  Y  U  L  G  L  F  F
Y  F  D  D  T  S  L  T  G  P  S  D
S  F  O  O  T  B  A  L  L  O  H  T
```

JUDO	RUGBY	CYCLING
GOLF	FOOTBALL	SWIMMING
TENNIS	BASEBALL	VOLLEYBALL
SOCCER	HOCKEY	BASKETBALL

Solution on page 211

WHAT IS YOUR FAVORITE FOOD?

Draw it and color it. If you don't know how to draw it, you can also write it down

We left this page blank so as not to interfere with the previous exercise.

If you don't do the exercise, feel free to use this page to draw or write whatever you like!

WHISPER TO LOUD

Repeat the same sentence at different volumes, starting with a whisper and ending loudly

Big brown bear

Big brown bear

Big brown bear

Big brown bear

Big brown bear

JOIN THE DOTS

Complete the dot-to-dot and color the
hidden drawing

Write the name of the hidden animal

....

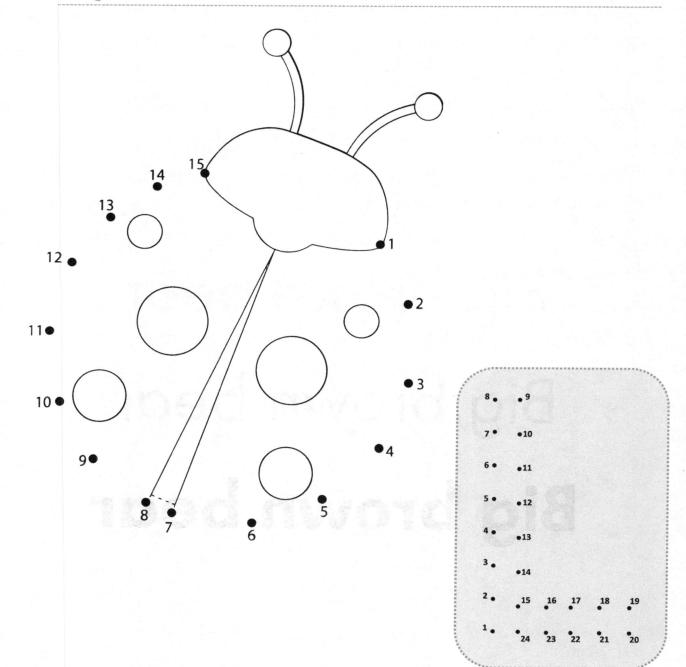

TRUE OR FALSE

Read the sentences and circle true (T) or false (F)

Trees are blue.   T / F

Grass is green.   T / F

Trees have branches.   T / F

Grass has petals.   T / F

Birds are mammals.   T / F

There are 365 days in a year.   T / F

Cats can speak English.   T / F

Each season lasts four months.   T / F

Chickens lay eggs.   T / F

Solution on page 212

WHAT TIME IS IT?

Look at the clocks, what time is it?
Write it down

Solution on page 213

DESIGN YOUR MUG

Draw, paint, and glue whatever you want to create your mug

We left this page blank so as not to interfere with the previous exercise.

If you don't do the exercise, feel free to use this page to draw or write whatever you like!

SHOWING EMOTION

Match the following images with the emotions they best capture. Then try showing the same emotion yourself

Love

Surprise

Anger

Boredom

Solution on page 214

WORD LIST

Place the words below in the corresponding list

Burger

Sandwich

Tango   Flamenco

Fencing

Swimming

Tennis   Tacos

Pizza

Basketball

Mambo   Soccer

Spaghetti

Reggaeton

Samba

Dances	Sports	Food

_____   _____   _____

_____   _____   _____

_____   _____   _____

_____   _____   _____

_____   _____   _____

Solution on page 215

SHOPPING LIST

Write down the shopping list for what we need to cook mac and cheese

TONGUE TWISTERS

Repeat each tongue twister 3 times, starting slowly and gradually increasing your speed

Fred fed Ted bread.

Black bug bleeds black blood.

Peter Piper picked a peck of pickled peppers.

COLOR THE LETTERS

Look at the word below and color the letters in it

COLORFUL

V C H U D A

U Y B F H M

N E A Z G P

O U X L E O

T R A U W B

K I H J L Q

Solution on page 216

DRAW THE EMOTION

Trace the word and draw the face of the emotion

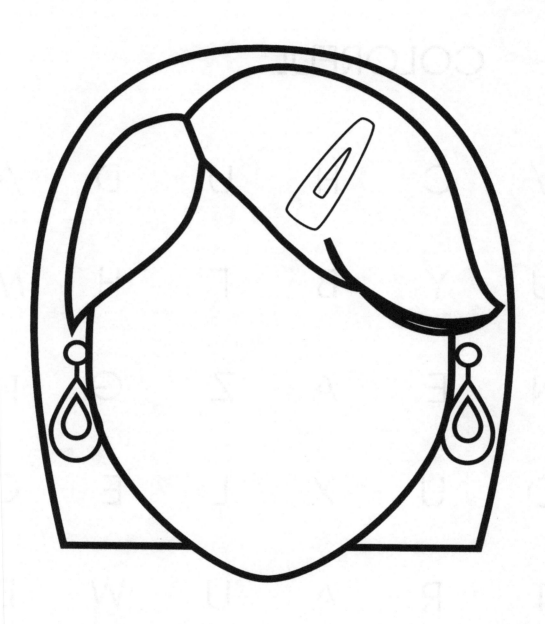

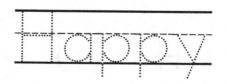

WRITTEN TIME

Draw a line to match each time to
each written time

9:00	Four O'clock
11:15	Quarter to six
4:00	Twelve O'clock
10:30	Nine O'clock
7:00	Half past one
5:45	Seven O'clock
12:00	Eight O'clock
5:00	Quarter past eleven
1:30	Five O'clock
8:00	Half past ten

Solution on page 217

IMITATION

Look at these gestures and mimic the same poses with your mouth. Repeat 3 times

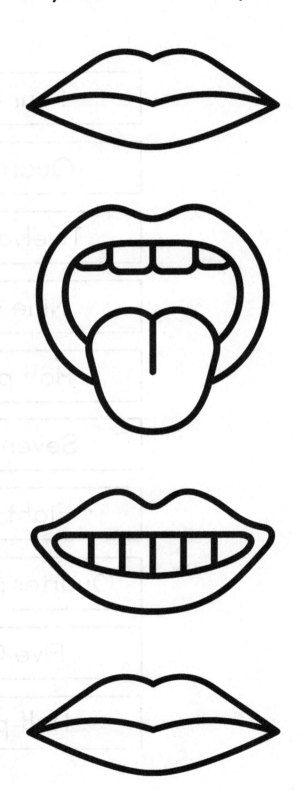

COLOR BY NUMBERS

Color the drawing with the color that corresponds to each number

 GREY

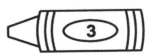 BLUE

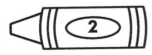 YELLOW

 ORANGE

We left this page blank so as not to interfere with the previous exercise.

If you don't do the exercise, feel free to use this page to draw or write whatever you like!

VISUAL SCANNING

Of the following objects, paint 5 of them in color

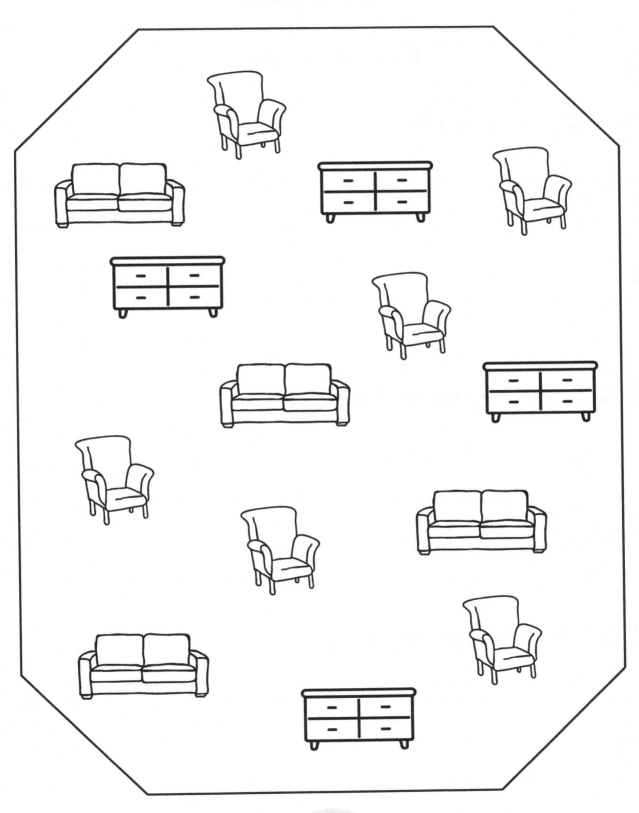

THOUGHT EXERCISE

Read the following sentences and
write down whatever comes to mind

Food and drink

Think of 5 fruits you like:

1 _____
2 _____
3 _____
4 _____
5 _____

Think of 4 international dishes:

1 _____
2 _____
3 _____
4 _____

Think of 3 non-alcoholic drinks:

1 _____
2 _____
3 _____

TRACE THE SHAPES

Carefully trace the shapes, then color
if you'd like

TRACE THE SHAPES

Carefully trace the shapes, then color
if you'd like

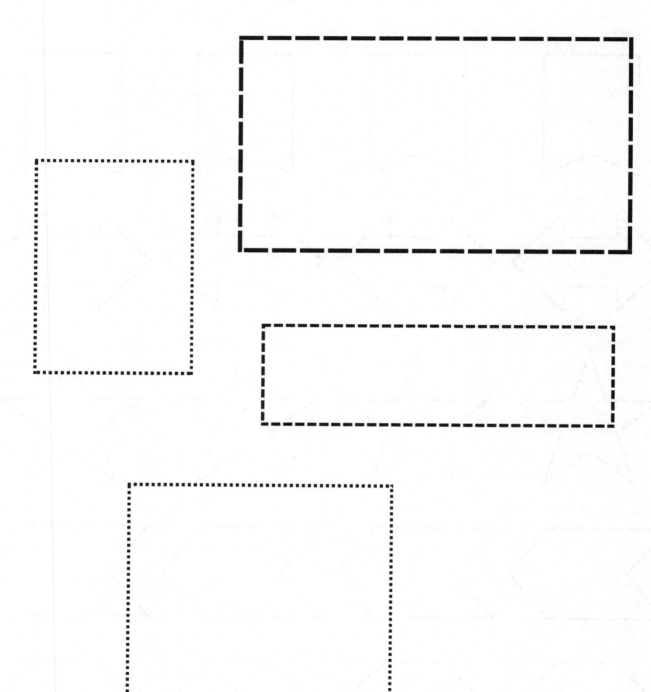

SHAPES CHALLENGE

Color 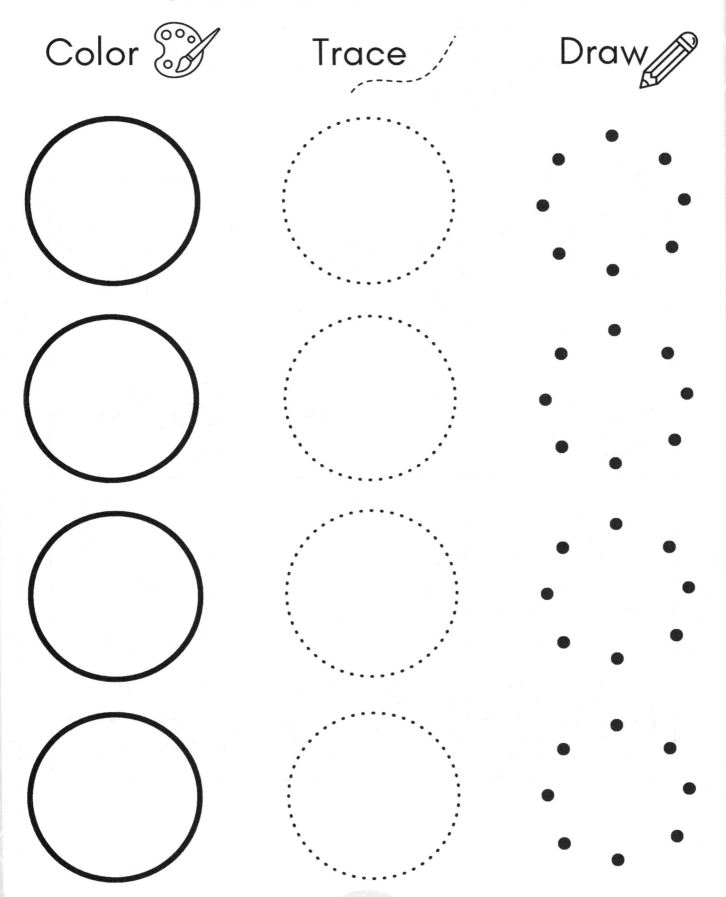 Trace   Draw

HALF OR NOT?

Color the happy face for shapes that are halves. Color the sad face for shapes that are not halves

Solution on page 218

FINISH THE PICTURE

Draw the other halves and color the pictures. Then, trace the words.

Leaf

Acorn

Pumpkin

Mushroom

CODING GAME

Observe the codes below, then copy them into the next box

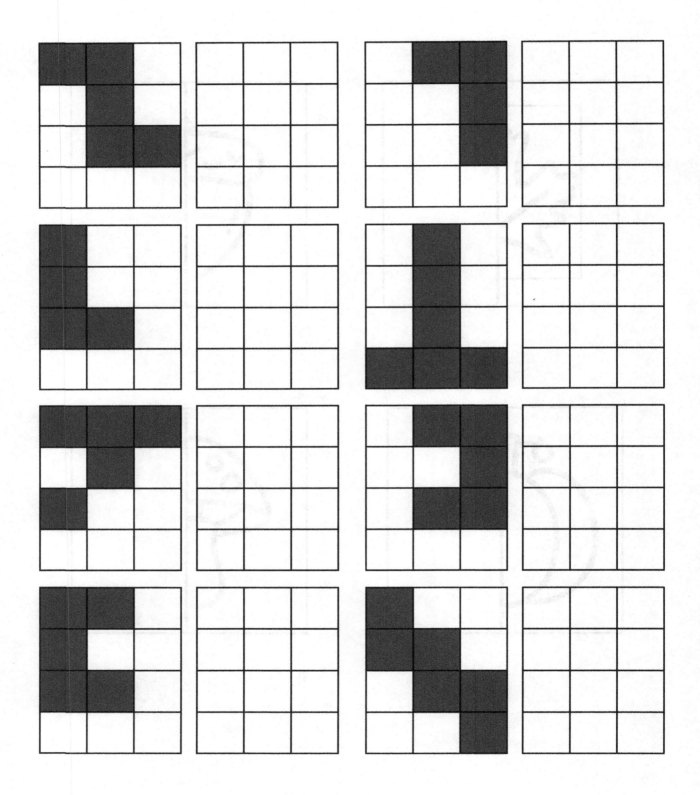

FIND AND TRACE

Find and trace the letters A, B, and C

Solution on page 219

WHAT'S THE WEATHER LIKE?

Connect the correct weather word to the matching image

Cloudy •

Sunny •

Snowy •

Rainy •

Windy •

Solution on page 220

COPY THE PATTERN

Observe the patterns on the left, draw the same pattern on the opposite box

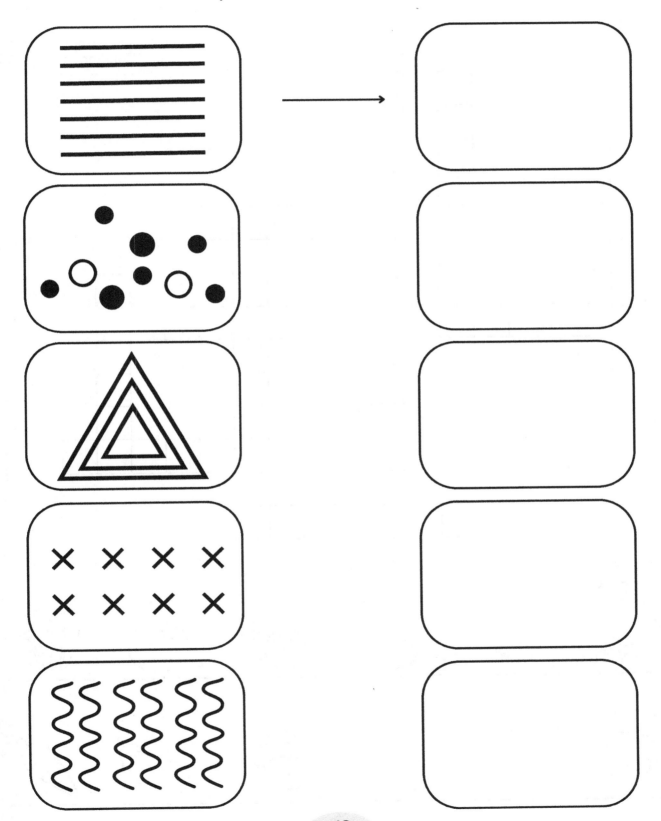

CROSSWORD - VEGETABLES

Complete the crossword using the given clues

🔍 Solution on page 221

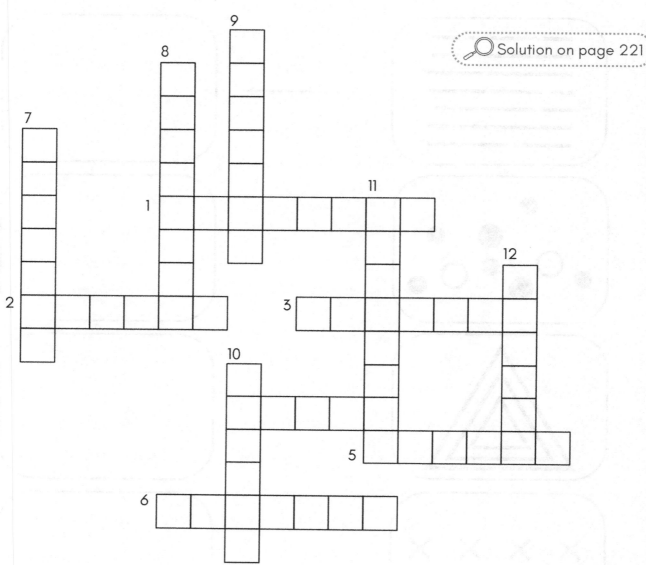

Across

1.

2.

3.

4.

5.

6.

Down

7.

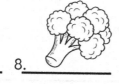

8.

9.

10.

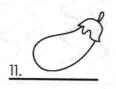

11.

12.

LOWERCASE WITH UPPERCASE

Connect lowercase and uppercase
with lines, then color matching pieces
the same color

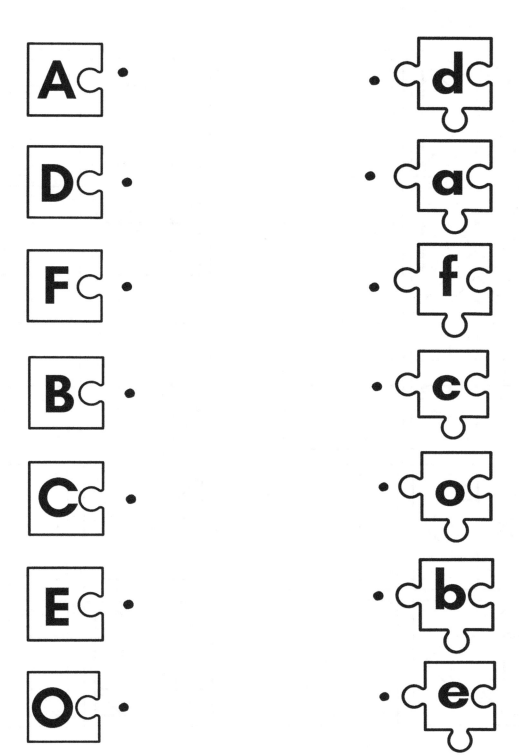

LINE CODING

Reply to the lines on the left by filling in
the empty boxes on the right

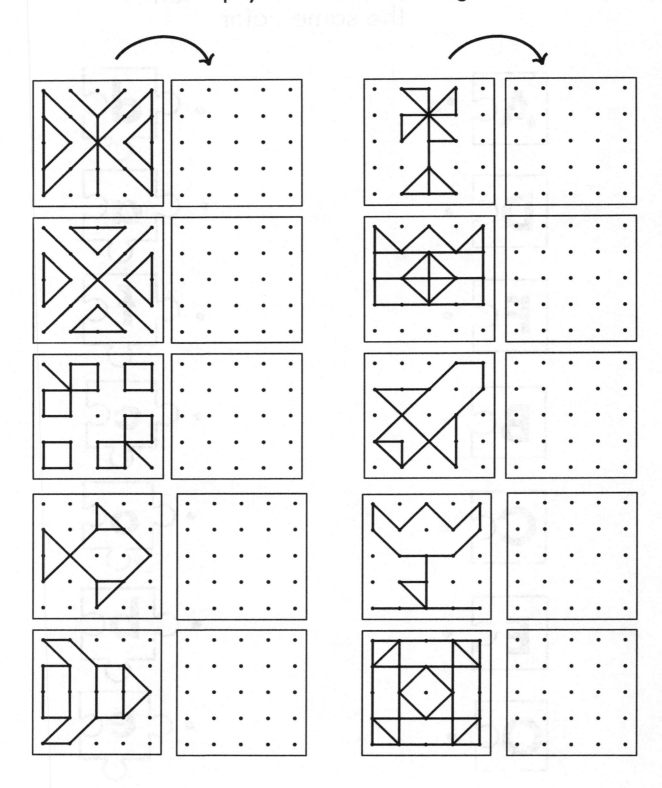

We left this page blank so as not to interfere with the previous exercise.

If you don't do the exercise, feel free to use this page to draw or write whatever you like!

WORD SEARCH - SPRING

Find the items listed below

```
R E D Y C N E B U N D B
A P A A S E I L M P U U
I K I T E S S A B I A T
N J S C P T I D R C P T
C A Y W G A R D E N A E
O N N L P N N F L I R R
A U G S E E B T L C T F
T U L I P A B A A N Y L
I O S U H O L D A I S Y
R A I N B O O T S H I H
G F I C H A O I T Y A U
B L O S S O M Y B U G G
```

KITE	NEST	DAISY	TULIP
GARDEN	RAINCOAT	BLOOM	PICNIC
UMBRELLA	RAINBOOTS	BLOSSOM	BUTTERFLY

Solution on page 222

MAZE CHALLENGE

Find the correct path to connect the
bee with the flowers

UNSCRAMBLE

Unscramble the letters to find the
words, then color the images

SOOBT

WNOS

OHCCTLAOE

THA

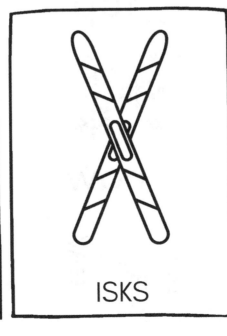

ISKS

PERILAFEC

Solution on page 223

MISSING LETTERS

Complete the following words with the missing letters

P T S W

_tar

_lum

_kip

_ram

_top

_wim

_rap

_now

_ray

_wan

_able

_hop

Solution on page 224

COLOR THE BALL

Carefully trace the lines, then color the
Christmas ball

We left this page blank so as not to interfere with the previous exercise.

If you don't do the exercise, feel free to use this page to draw or write whatever you like!

COUNT THE OBJECTS - EASTER

Count how many objects there are of
each and write them down

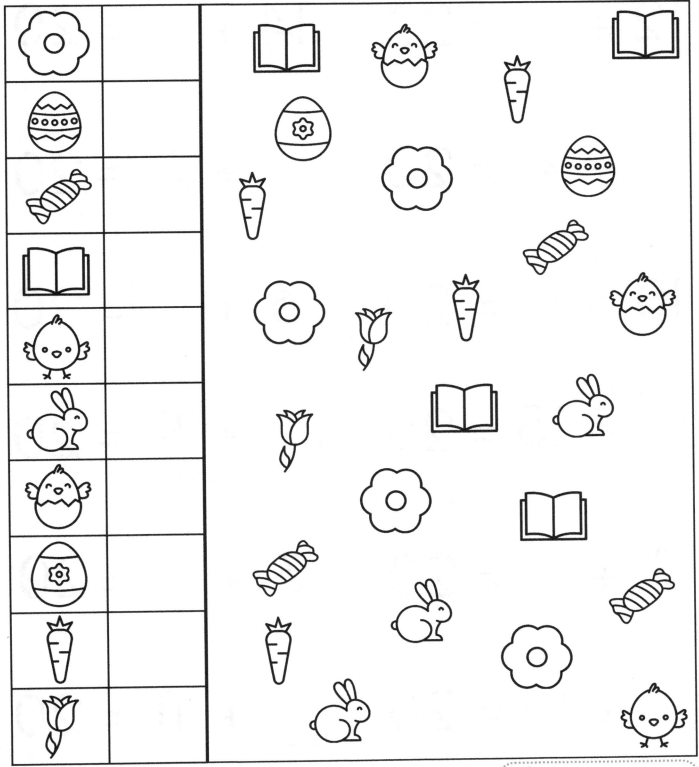

Solution on page 225

FRIENDS OF NUMBER 20

Complete the following problems to
show the number 20

$12 +$ ☐ $= 20$ $14 +$ ☐ $= 20$

☐ $+ 4 = 20$ ☐ $+ 5 = 20$

$10 +$ ☐ $= 20$ $6 +$ ☐ $= 20$

☐ $+ 13 = 20$ ☐ $+ 9 = 20$

$7 +$ ☐ $= 20$ $3 +$ ☐ $= 20$

☐ $+ 15 = 20$ ☐ $+ 11 = 20$

Solution on page 226

SUM THE DICE

Fill the right number box with the number on the dice

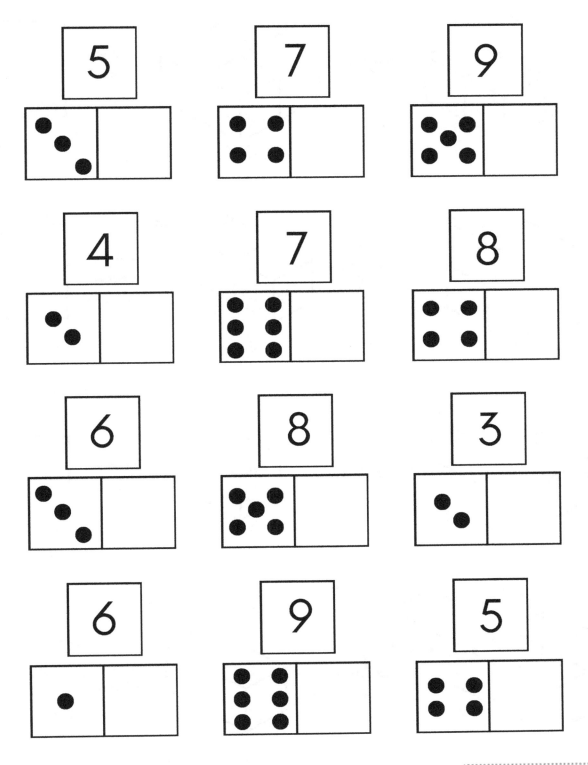

Solution on page 227

FIND THE SUM

Count the cubes and write the sum in the box

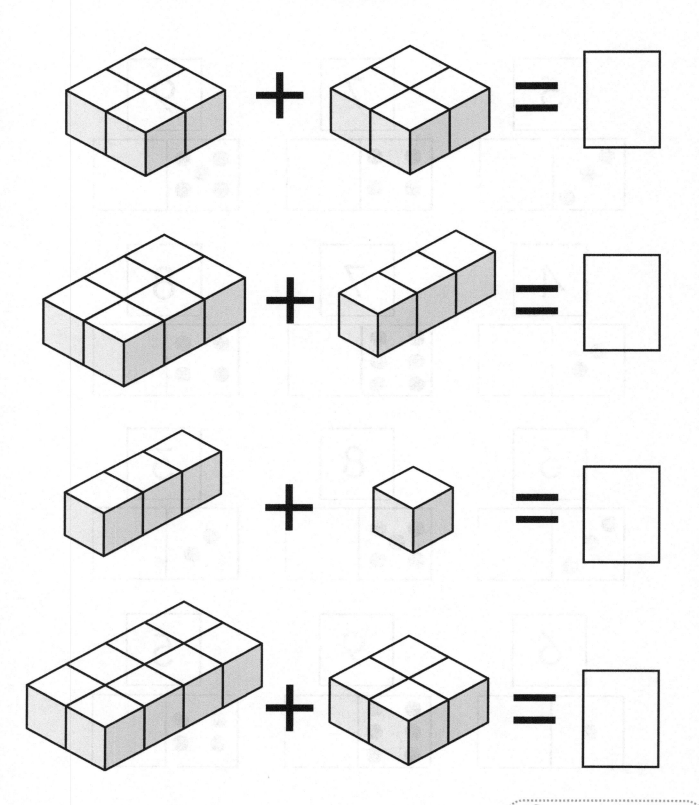

Solution on page 228

EMOJI CHALLENGE

Copy each hand emoji with your hands

CONNECT THE DOTS

Trace the lines to connect the dots

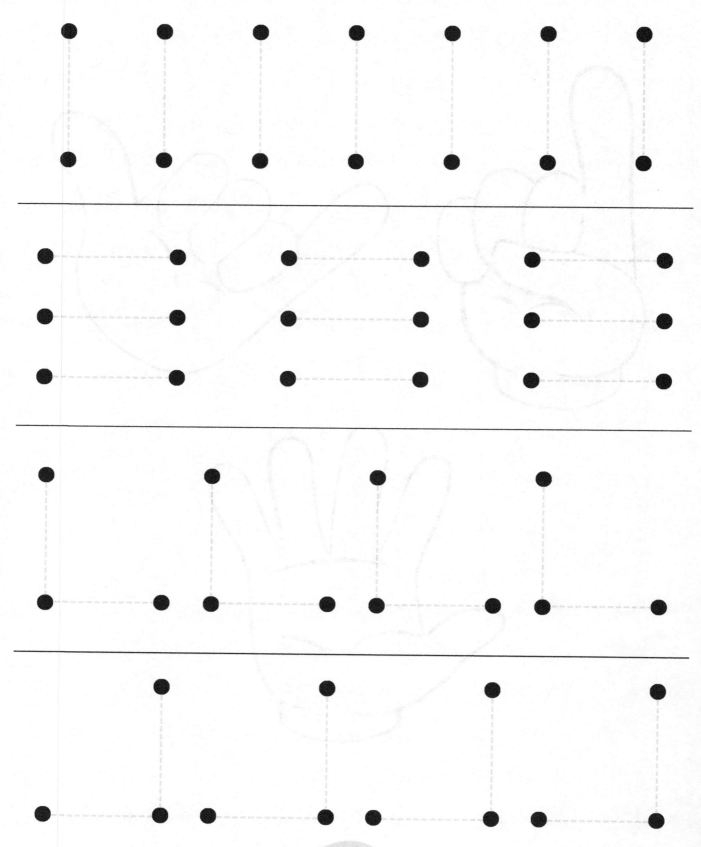

ODD MAN OUT

Below are lists of different topics.
Circle the word that does not belong
to the group

SEPTEMBER

APRIL

BOOTS

MAY

WALL

WINDOW

SOCKS

FLOOR

COFFEE

WATER

ORANGES

TEA

BASKETBALL

SOCCER

SANDALS

SURFING

SISTER

MOTHER

SHAMPOO

FATHER

LONDON

PARIS

BEACH

ISTANBUL

Solution on page 229

DRAW THE HANDS ON THE CLOCK TO SHOW THE TIME

Seven o'clock

Four o'clock

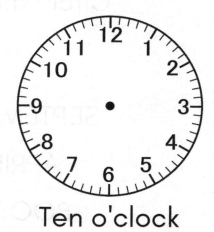
Ten o'clock

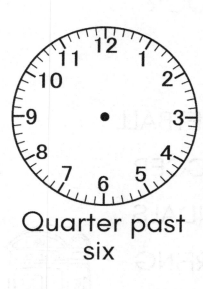
Quarter past six

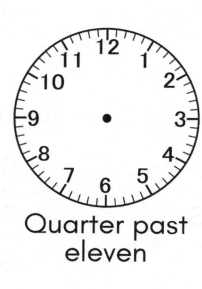
Quarter past eleven

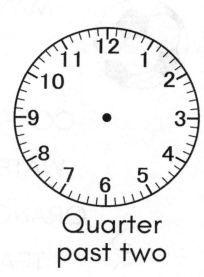
Quarter past two

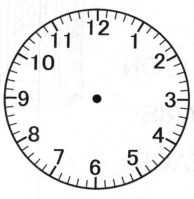
Half past nine

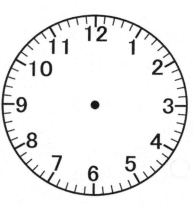
Half past six

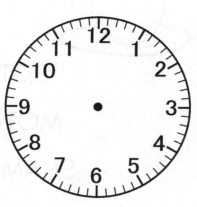
Half past three

Solution on page 230

WHAT JOB IS IT?

Assign the activities listed below to the correct person

Taxi Driver (T)   Chef (C)   Architect (A)

_____ Setting up menus

_____ Visits buildings under construction

_____ Makes car rides more comfortable

_____ Accompanies people to their homes

_____ Tasting dishes before serving

_____ Works in a car

_____ Always thinking of new recipes

_____ Works on projects

_____ Constructs buildings

_____ Charges by the minute

_____ Has a good sense of aesthetic

_____ Prepping the kitchen before meal times

_____ Works sitting down

_____ Designs building plans

_____ Overseeing kitchen staff

Solution on page 231

WORD SEARCH - FARM ANIMALS

Find the items listed below

```
R  A  G  E  S  R  A  B  B  B  I  T  A
B  H  I  O  M  I  O  K  P  V  A  S
D  X  E  R  A  S  A  C  O  W  L  D
U  O  H  L  A  T  C  C  E  R  A  O
C  T  O  C  O  M  E  I  T  I  D  N
K  I  R  C  H  W  E  M  O  T  K  K
N  R  S  S  E  A  L  G  O  O  S  E
R  C  E  H  N  V  A  A  V  G  F  Y
E  U  W  V  E  C  H  I  C  K  L  E
P  I  G  K  T  L  K  C  O  T  U  M
B  V  T  E  P  L  S  H  E  E  P  N
E  D  O  V  E  T  I  R  E  L  F  R
```

RABBIT	SHEEP	PIG	CHICK
DONKEY	GOAT	COW	DOVE
GOOSE	DUCK	HEN	HORSE

Solution on page 232

SCISSOR SKILLS

Color in this girl and cut along the
wavy lines of her hair

We left this page blank so as not to interfere with the previous exercise.

If you don't do the exercise, feel free to use this page to draw or write whatever you like!

MATCH THE HOMOPHONES

Highlight the word that names each picture

TWO
TO

PEAR
PARE

FLOWER
FLOUR

BEAR
BARE

CELL
SELL

KNIGHT
NIGHT

MEET
MEAT

ATE
EIGHT

Solution on page 233

WHISPER TO LOUD

Repeat the same sentence at different volumes, starting with a whisper and ending loudly

Big dog barks

Big dog barks

Big dog barks

Big dog barks

Big dog barks

LETTERS IN YOUR NAME

Color the letters that are in your first and last name.

 Write your first and last name:

V   C   H   U   D   A

U   Y   B   F   H   M

N   E   A   Z   G   P

O   U   X   L   E   Z

T   R   A   U   W   B

K   I   H   J   S   Q

TRUE OR FALSE

Read the sentences and circle true (T)
or false (F)

The capital of Canada is Ottawa.   T / F

Octopuses have eight legs.   T / F

Thomas Edison invented the light bulb.   T / F

The Mona Lisa was painted by Leonardo
da Vinci.   T / F

The Statue of Liberty was a gift from
France to the United States.   T / F

A triangle has three sides.   T / F

Watermelon grows on trees.   T / F

The shortest month of the year is
December.   T / F

Solution on page 234

ODD ONE OUT

Look at the grid below. There is a shape that does not match. Circle it

A	A	A	A	A
A	A	A	A	A
A	A	A	4	A
A	A	A	A	A
A	A	A	A	A

Solution on page 235

LETTER COMBINATIONS

Circle the 3 combinations that are
identical to the one in the rectangle

ALNM

NLMA	NAML	ANML	LANM
LNAM	LAMN	NMAL	AMLN
ANLM	ALNM	LMNA	NLAM
MLNA	BNMA	MALN	LNMA
ALNM	MANB	ALNM	BNMA
MANL	AMNL	NMLA	LBMA
MNLA	MNBH	MNAL	BLNM
MLAN	BANM	ALMN	MBLN

Solution on page 236

I'M LOOKING FOR THAT PERSON

Think of someone you know who has
the following characteristics and
complete the table

I'M LOOKING FOR SOMEONE WHO...	NAME
Works out a lot	
Cooks very well	
Has a pet	
Speaks 3 languages	
Has siblings	

TONGUE TWISTERS

Repeat each tongue twister 3 times,
starting slowly and gradually increasing
your speed

Red lorry, yellow lorry.

She sells seashells by the seashore.

How much wood would a
woodchuck chuck if a woodchuck
could chuck wood?

HEALTHY OR UNHEALTHY

Read the habits and sort them into
healthy or unhealthy habits

Running

Workout

Eat vegetables

Reading books

Watching too much TV

Drink soda

Procrastinating

Not enough sleep

Drink water

Walk daily

Sleep all day

Eat fast food

HEALTHY HABITS

UNHEALTHY HABITS

IMITATION

Look at these gestures and mimic the same poses with your eyes. Repeat 2 times

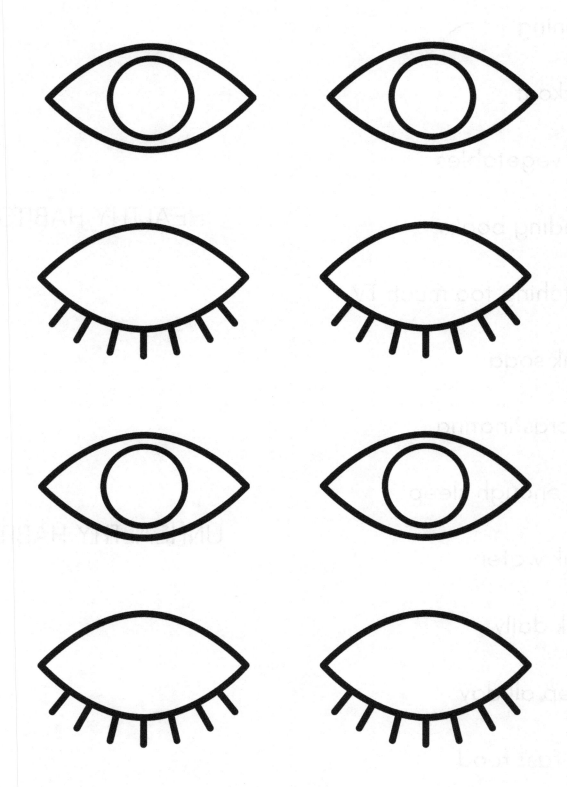

COLOR BY NUMBERS

Color the drawing with the color that
corresponds to each number

1 — ORANGE
2 — YELLOW
3 — GREEN
4 — BLUE

We left this page blank so as not to interfere with the previous exercise.

If you don't do the exercise, feel free to use this page to draw or write whatever you like!

WRITE A POSTCARD

Write a message on this postcard and address it to a family member or a friend

NUMBER OF OBJECTS

Trace and count the objects

3   Three

8   Eight

10   Ten

4   Four

VISUAL SCANNING

Of the following objects, paint 5 of
them in color

TRACE AND COPY SHAPES

Trace the shapes, then draw your own

COLOR THE SHAPES

Color the geometric shapes Green
Color the organic shapes Orange

MIRROR SHAPE

Draw the other half of each shape

TRACE THE LETTERS

Carefully trace the letters

Aa Bb Cc Dd Ee

Ff Gg Hh Ii Jj

Kk Ll Mm Nn Oo

Pp Qq Rr Ss Tt

Uu Vv Ww Xx

Yy Zz

WHICH IS WHICH ON THANKSGIVING?

Connect the correct word to the matching image

Turkey •   •

Pumpkin pie •   •

Family •   •

Football •   •

Corn •   •

Solution on page 237

MAZE CHALLENGE

Find the correct path to connect these
animals with their favorite food

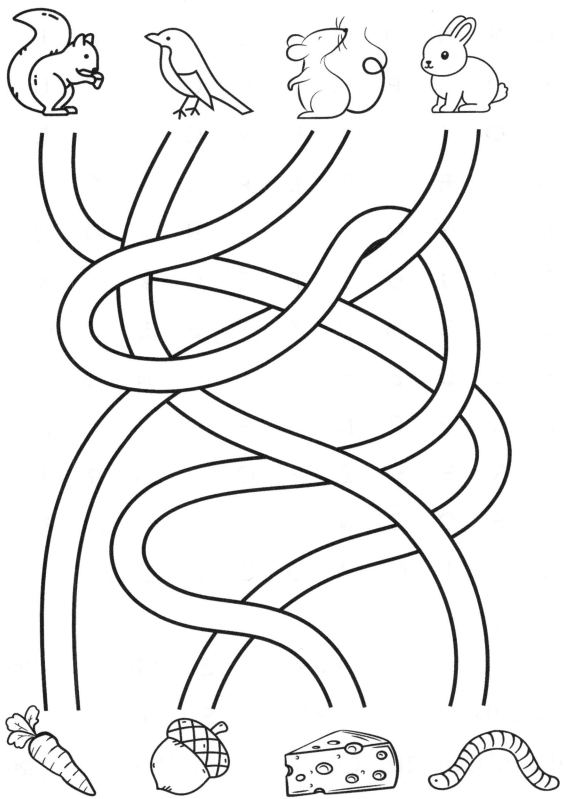

WORD SEARCH - WINTER

Find the items listed below

```
C  S  N  O  W  C  S  O  C  O  L  D
H  N  L  P  M  H  C  O  L  T  U  U
J  O  I  C  I  U  A  O  F  I  R  S
S  W  E  A  T  E  R  O  L  C  I  N
N  B  Y  M  T  S  F  N  A  D  C  O
G  A  J  U  E  F  O  C  K  I  K  W
L  L  B  M  N  T  T  E  E  S  O  M
E  L  D  B  S  K  I  I  N  G  T  A
R  R  P  R  N  S  E  C  T  S  E  N
F  R  E  E  Z  E  C  T  O  R  I  S
D  F  C  O  N  F  O  V  L  A  K  N
H  O  T  C  H  O  C  O  L  A  T  E
```

SNOWMAN	SNOW	SWEATER	SKIING
SNOWBALL	COLD	SCARF	FLAKE
HOT CHOCOLATE	COAT	MITTENS	FREEZE

Solution on page 238

UNSCRAMBLE

Unscramble the letters to find the
words, then color the images

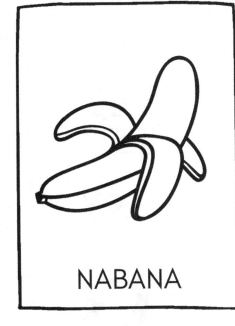

NABANA

PPLEA

APERG

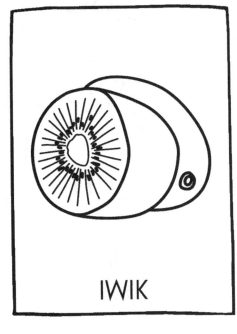

IWIK

ERRWABTRSY

REAP

Solution on page 239

MISSING LETTERS

Complete the following words with the missing letters

M   N   D   P   T   S

_ut

_ad

_oy

_ap

_op

_ad

_ot

_um

_un

_it

_in

_ig

Solution on page 240

DESIGN YOUR NOTEBOOK

Draw, paint, and glue whatever you
want to create your notebook

TASKS TO DO TODAY

We left this page blank so as not to interfere with the previous exercise.

If you don't do the exercise, feel free to use this page to draw or write whatever you like!

CROSSWORD - CLOTHES

Complete the crossword using the given clues

Solution on page 241

Across

 1.

 2.

 3.

 4.

 5.

 6.

Down

 7.

 8.

 9.

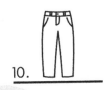 10.

 11.

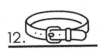 12.

UNSCRAMBLE

Unscramble the letters to find the words

ANTU

_____

SNO

_____

UCLEN

_____

SESTIR

_____

METHOR

_____

FRETHA

_____

BOERTHR

_____

GARNDAP

_____

GRMANDA

_____

SBLINISG

_____

CUONISS

_____

DUAGHRET

_____

Solution on page 242

COUNT THE OBJECTS - HALLOWEEN

Count how many objects there are of
each and write them down

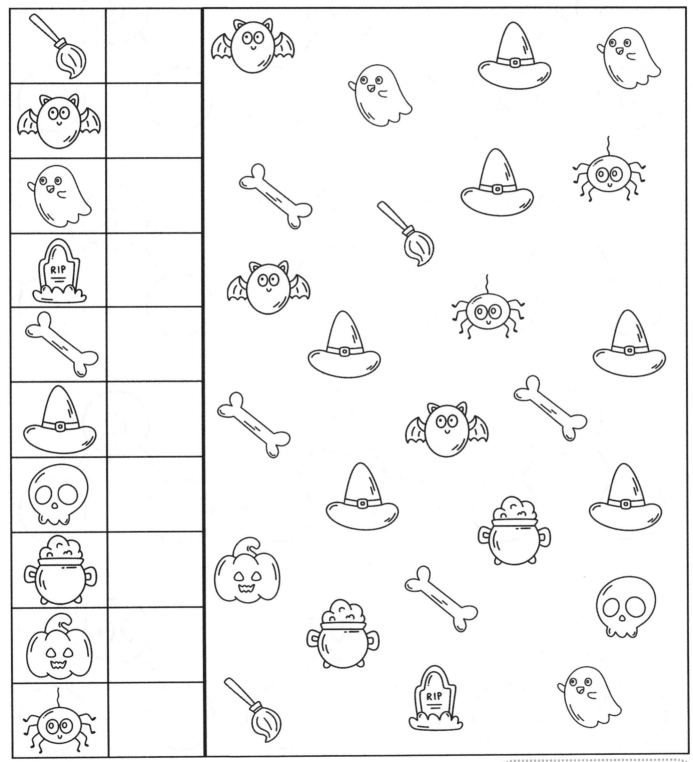

Solution on page 243

DECOMPOSITION

Break these numbers down into tens
and units

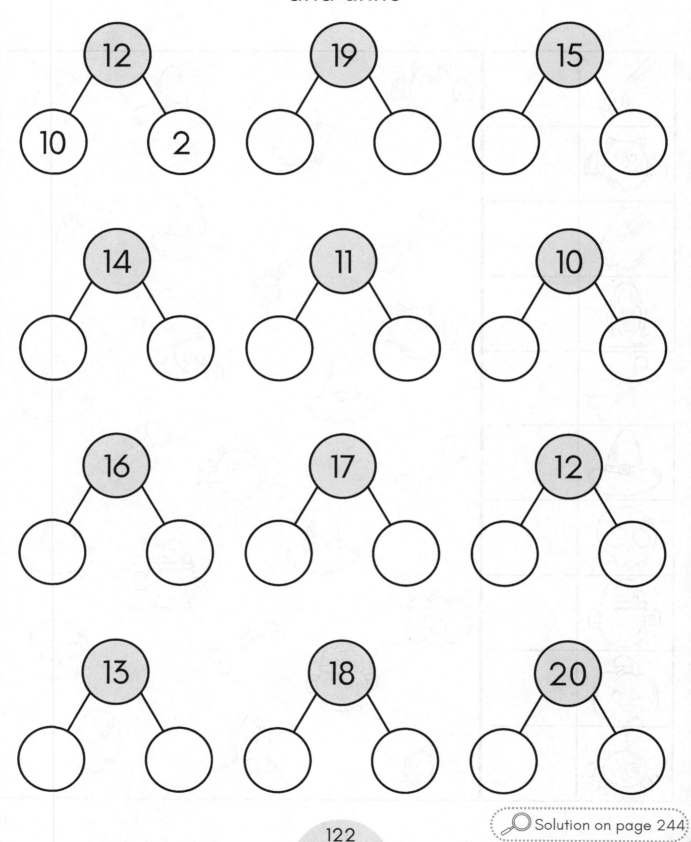

Solution on page 244

MATCHING ADDITION

Add up these numbers and match the
result with the numbers on the right

 2 + 3

16

 9 + 7

12

 8 + 5

5

 7 + 5

13

Solution on page 245

STARS ADDITION

Add up these numbers and find the answer in the stars

10 + 12 = _____   19 + 4 = _____

9 + 9 = _____   24 + 3 = _____

21 + 5 = _____   8 + 11 = _____

9 + 11 = _____   7 + 7 = _____

Solution on page 246

SUM THE DICE

Fill the right number box with the number on the dice

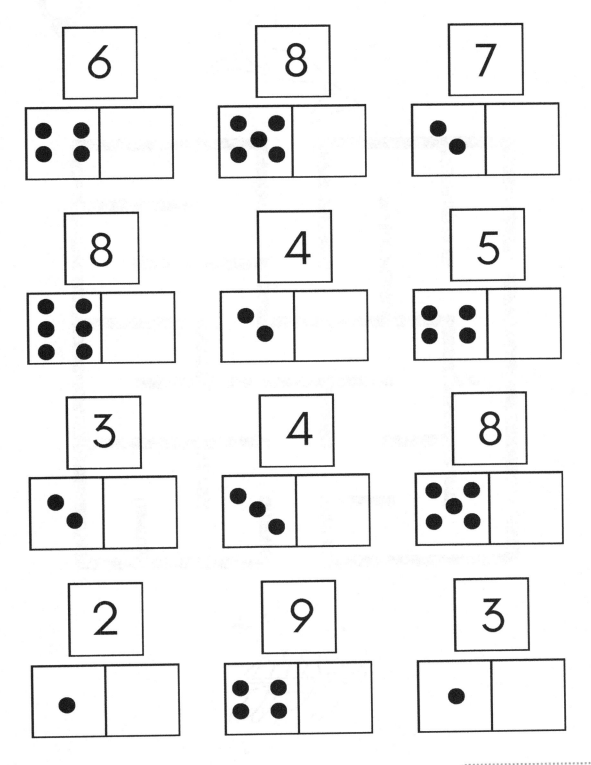

Solution on page 247

MAZE CHALLENGE

Find the correct path to connect the
dolphin with the turtle

WHISPER TO LOUD

Repeat the same sentence at different volumes, starting with a whisper and ending loudly

Funny bunny hops

Funny bunny hops

Funny bunny hops

Funny bunny hops

Funny bunny hops

MATCH THE HOMOPHONES

Highlight the word that names each picture

☀	SUN
	SON

1	WON
	ONE

🐝	BE
	BEE

🌊	SEE
	SEA

4	FOR
	FOUR

⛵	SAIL
	SALE

✍	RIGHT
	WRITE

👨	MAIL
	MALE

Solution on page 248

DRAW THE EMOTION

Trace the word and draw the face of the emotion

Sad

TONGUE TWISTERS

Repeat each tongue twister 3 times, starting slowly and gradually increasing your speed

Six sticky skeletons.

Betty Botter bought some butter.

I scream, you scream, we all scream for ice cream.

WHAT JOB IS IT?

Assign the activities listed below to the correct person

Doctor (D)   Teacher (T)   Firefighter (F)

_____ Grading tests

_____ Risks their life working

_____ Puts out fires

_____ Works in a white coat

_____ Cares for patients

_____ Wears heavy gear for work

_____ Preparing lesson materials

_____ Wears a helmet on a daily basis

_____ Prescribes medication for patients

_____ Needs to be in good shape

_____ Assigning homework

_____ Measuring students' progress

_____ Visits patients

_____ Explaining the lesson

_____ Has studied the human body

Solution on page 249

SHADOW MATCHING
Draw a line from each item to its matching shadow

Solution on page 250

ODD ONE OUT

Look at the grid below. There is a
shape that does not match. Circle it

7	7	7	7	7
7	7	7	7	7
7	7	7	7	7
T	7	7	7	7
7	7	7	7	7

Solution on page 251

ODD MAN OUT

Below are lists of different pieces of clothing. Circle the word that does not belong to the group

HAT

BOOTS

SHOES

SLIPPERS

BAG

SUIT

DRESS

BLOUSE

COAT

T-SHIRT

JACKET

SWEATER

JACKET

BLOUSE

JEANS

SHIRT

EARRINGS

NECKLACE

BRACELET

BAG

PANTS

SHIRT

WATCH

PAJAMAS

Solution on page 252

TRUE OR FALSE

Read the sentences and circle true (T)
or false (F)

There are eleven months in a year.   T / F

Penguins can fly.   T / F

November is the last month of the year.   T / F

Giraffes have short necks.   T / F

The sun is smaller than a soccer ball.   T / F

Apples are a type of fruit.   T / F

There are stars in the sky.   T / F

Ice cream is typically served hot.   T / F

Solution on page 253

DRAW THE HANDS ON THE CLOCK TO SHOW THE TIME

Two o'clock

Half past five

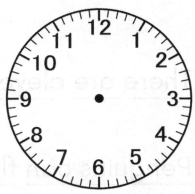

Quarter past one

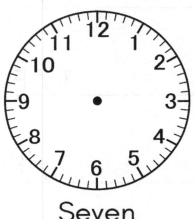

Seven o'clock

Quarter past eight

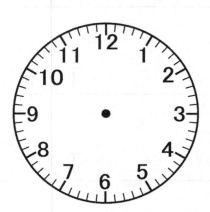

Ten o'clock

Half past eleven

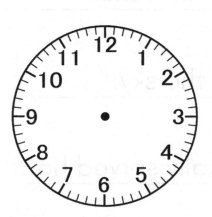

Nine o'clock

Quarter to six

Solution on page 254

COLOR THE LETTERS

Look at the word below and color the letters in it

 MANDALA

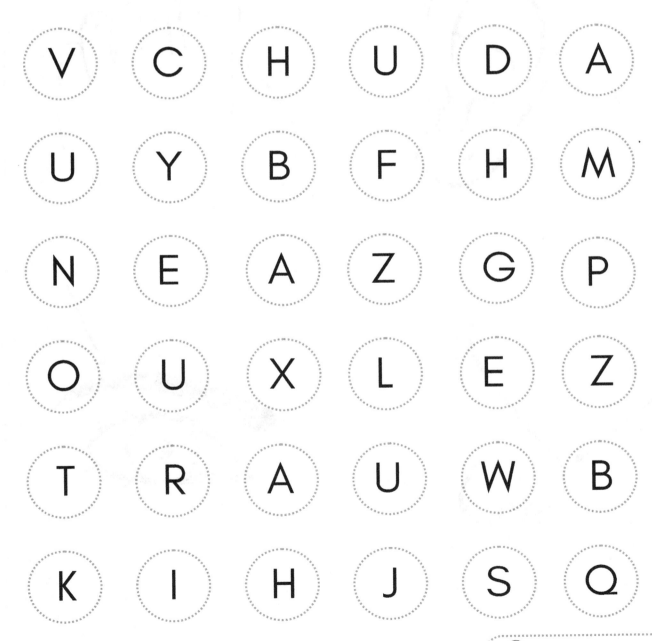

V	C	H	U	D	A
U	Y	B	F	H	M
N	E	A	Z	G	P
O	U	X	L	E	Z
T	R	A	U	W	B
K	I	H	J	S	Q

Solution on page 255

BODY POINTING

With your index finger, point to the part of the body indicated in each picture

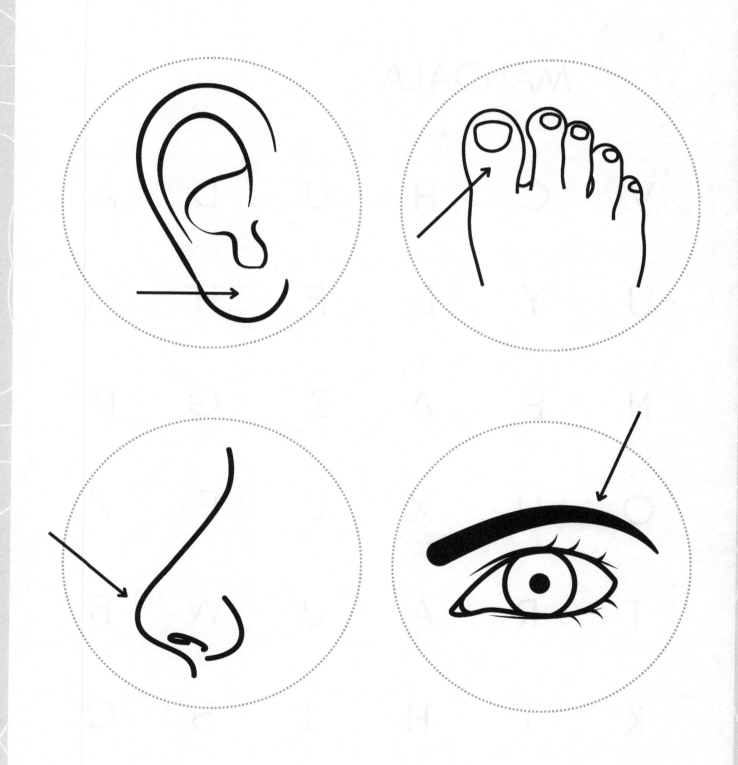

We left this page blank so as not to interfere with the previous exercise.

If you don't do the exercise, feel free to use this page to draw or write whatever you like!

I LIKE OR I DON'T LIKE

Read these activities and categorize them based on whether you like them or not

Sleeping

Being with family

Being alone

Eating healthy

Watching TV

Browsing social media

Cooking

Doing outdoor activities

Scrubbing the dishes

I LIKE

I DON'T LIKE

THOUGHT EXERCISE

Read the following sentences and write down whatever comes to mind

Leisure Activities

Think of 5 hobbies you enjoy:

1
_____
2
_____
3
_____
4
_____
5
_____

Think of 4 movies you like:

1
_____
2
_____
3
_____
4
_____

Think of 3 books you have read:

1
_____
2
_____
3
_____

RECOGNIZE THE NUMBER

Read and respond to the following
exercises to recognize the number 5

Make a 5 with your fingers

Trace the 5 with your
finger

Count the petals
that the flower has

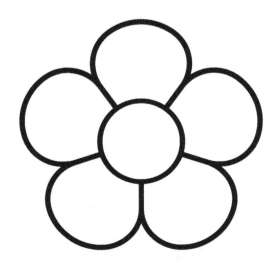

TRACE THE SHAPES

Carefully trace the shapes, then color
if you'd like

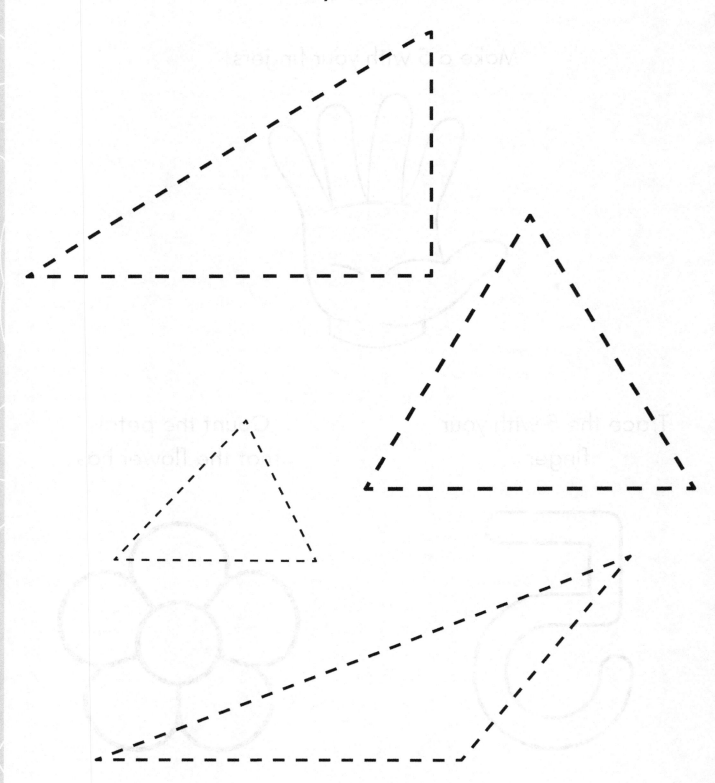

TRACE AND COPY SHAPES

Trace the shapes, then draw your own

SYMMETRY

Draw the line of symmetry on each shape

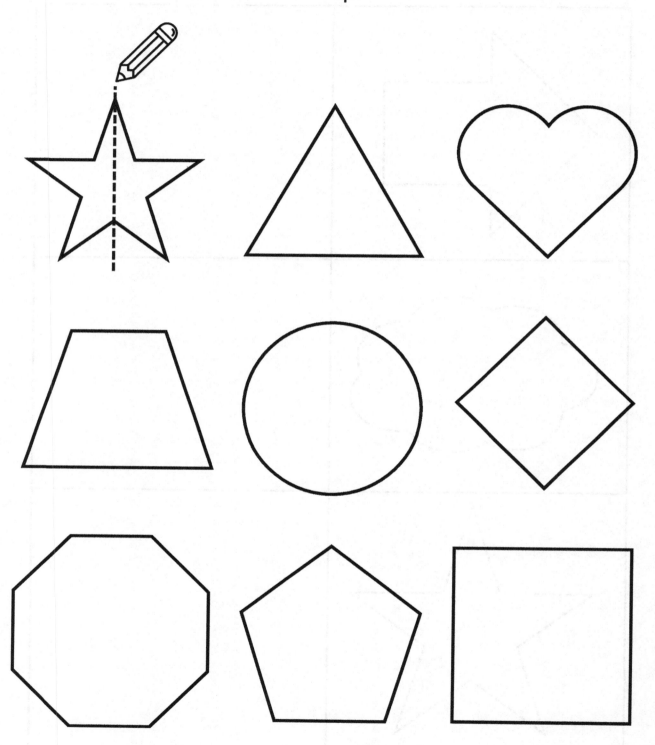

FINISH THE PICTURE

Draw the other halves and color the pictures. Then, trace the words

Heart

Teddy bear

Gift

Flowers

LOWERCASE WITH UPPERCASE

Connect lowercase and uppercase
with lines, then color matching pieces
the same color

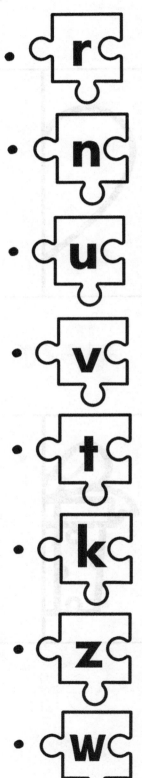

N ·

R ·

K ·

T ·

V ·

W ·

U ·

z ·

RECREATE THE PATTERN

Observe the patterns below, recreate them in the next box

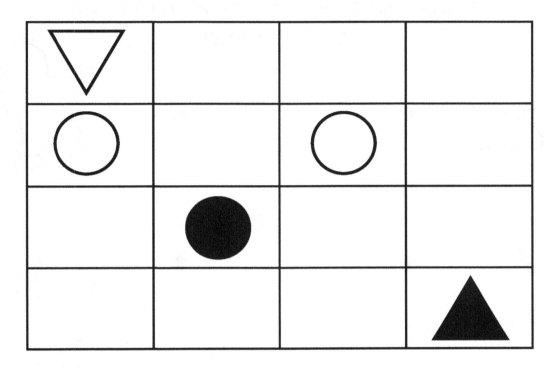

Your turn!

WHICH IS WHICH ON CHRISTMAS?

Connect the correct word to the matching image

Santa Claus ●

Gift ●

Gingerbread man ●

Decoration ●

Sleigh ●

Solution on page 256

WHAT COMES NEXT?

Look at the sequence and identify which patterned block goes in the fourth spot, then mark it

1

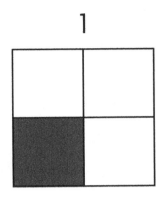

2

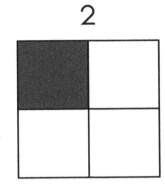

3

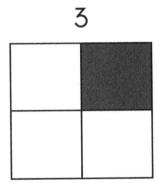

A

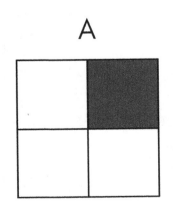

B

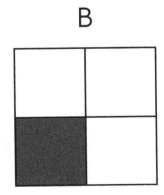

C

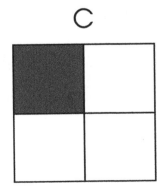

D

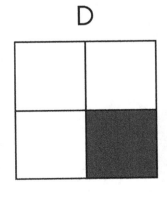

Solution on page 257

TRACE THE NUMBERS

Carefully trace the numbers

80   79   78   77

76   75   74   73

72   71   70   69

68   67   66   65

64   63

CROSSWORD - SEA ANIMALS

Complete the crossword using the given clues

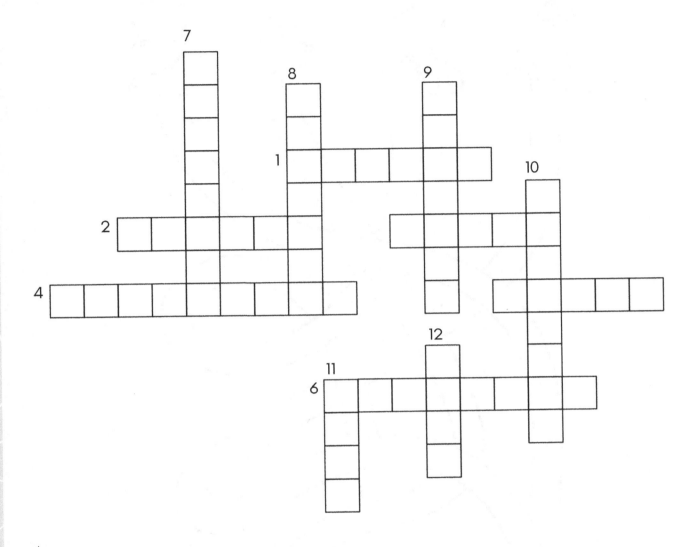

Across

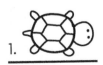 1.

 2.

 3.

 4.

 5.

 6.

Down

 7.

 8.

 9.

 10.

 11.

 12.

Solution on page 258

MAZE CHALLENGE

Find the correct path to connect these workers with their workplace

WORD SEARCH - FAMILY MEMBERS

Find the items listed below

```
S  Y  F  A  T  H  E  R  T  U  R  Q
M  O  E  E  A  D  O  A  U  N  T  A
S  R  N  C  M  D  A  A  N  C  R  G
F  P  C  C  O  D  O  C  C  L  R  R
G  T  A  B  T  U  O  H  L  E  N  A
R  H  D  R  H  I  S  T  E  R  N  N
A  E  E  O  E  N  V  I  S  E  N  D
N  R  N  T  R  N  I  X  N  T  R  M
D  V  T  H  A  D  T  C  C  H  R  A
P  P  I  E  O  S  I  S  T  E  R  V
A  V  S  R  A  D  Z  C  G  R  R  E
S  D  A  U  G  H  T  E  R  O  H  T
```

SON	FATHER	COUSIN	GRANDPA
AUNT	MOTHER	BROTHER	GRANDMA
UNCLE	SISTER	PARENTS	DAUGHTER

Solution on page 259

MISSING LETTERS

Complete the following words with the
missing letters

B C F G H

_ish

_ird

_arm

_orn

_and

_ift

_amp

_olf

_arp

_alf

_ork

_unk

Solution on page 260

CONNECT THE DOTS

Trace the lines to connect the dots

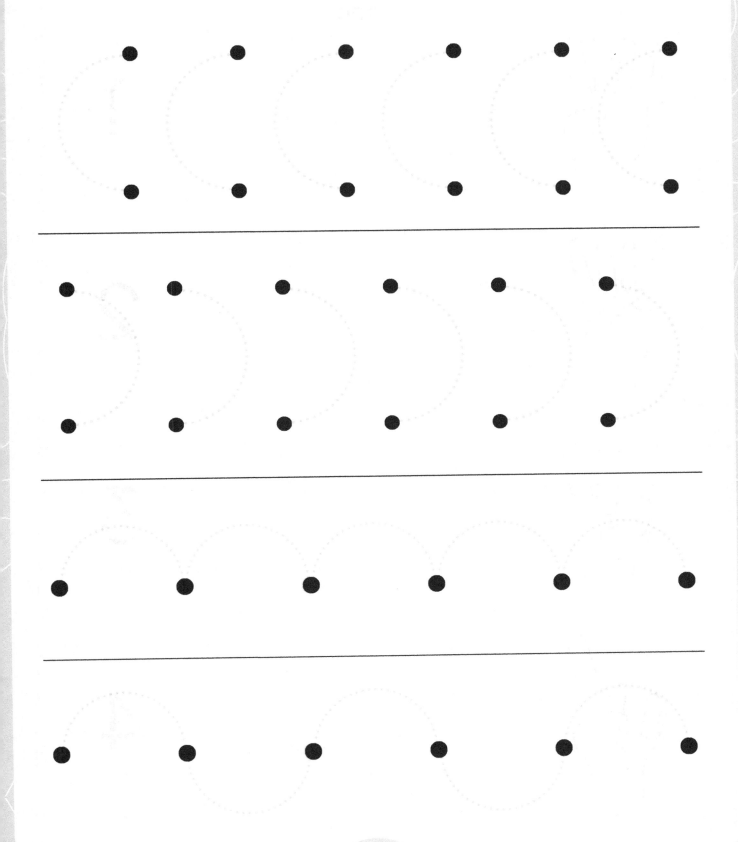

NUMBERS AND FINGERS

Find the matching number to each hand

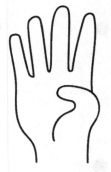

1

2

3

4

DESIGN YOUR CUPCAKE

Draw, paint, and glue whatever you
want to create your cupcake

We left this page blank so as not to interfere with the previous exercise.

If you don't do the exercise, feel free to use this page to draw or write whatever you like!

UNSCRAMBLE

Unscramble the letters to find the words, then color the images. Hint! Look at the monument, in which city is it located?

ONABLCEAR

SAPRI

OARM

WNE ROYK

NOODNL

RIEVRAR
AYMA

Solution on page 261

SHADOW MATCHING

Draw a line from each item to its matching shadow

Solution on page 262

COUNT THE OBJECTS - CHRISTMAS

Count how many objects there are of
each and write them down

Solution on page 263

FRIENDS OF NUMBER 10

Complete the following problems to
show the number 10

$8 + \boxed{} = 10$ $\qquad$ $0 + \boxed{} = 10$

$\boxed{} + 6 = 10$ $\qquad$ $\boxed{} + 9 = 10$

$2 + \boxed{} = 10$ $\qquad$ $7 + \boxed{} = 10$

$\boxed{} + 4 = 10$ $\qquad$ $\boxed{} + 5 = 10$

$10 + \boxed{} = 10$ $\qquad$ $3 + \boxed{} = 10$

$\boxed{} + 5 = 10$ $\qquad$ $\boxed{} + 1 = 10$

Solution on page 264

STARS ADDITION

Add up these numbers and find the
answer in the stars

31 + 2 = ___   10 + 5 = ___

20 + 5 = ___   9 + 2 = ___

19 + 7 = ___   7 + 10 = ___

17 + 3 = ___   13 + 3 = ___

Solution on page 265

MISSING NUMBERS

Fill each shape with the missing numbers from 31 to 50

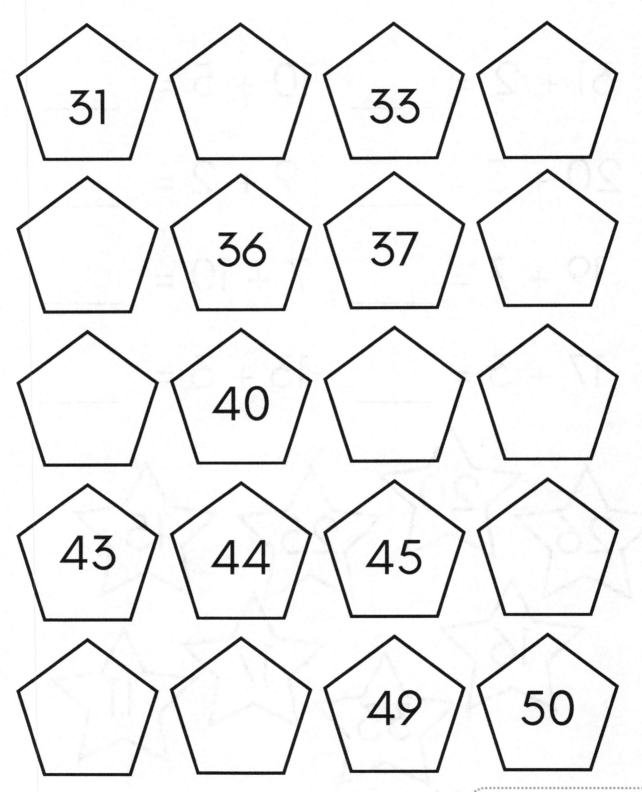

31   33

36   37

40

43   44   45

49   50

Solution on page 266

COUNT TO 100

Fill in the missing numbers and count to 100

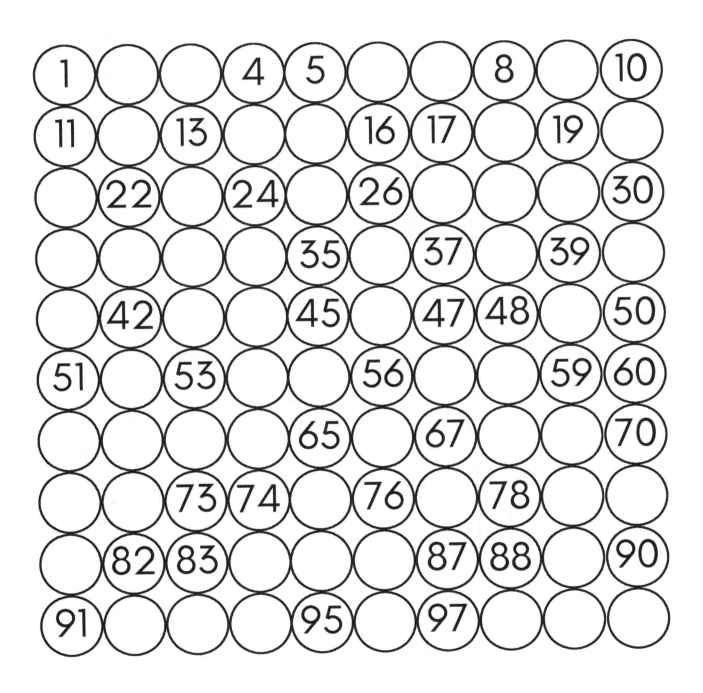

Solution on page 267

COLOR THE PORTIONS

Color the portions to represent the fraction

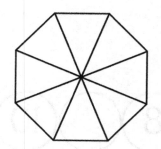

$$\frac{3}{8}$$

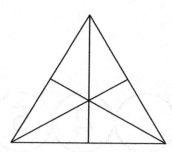

$$\frac{1}{6}$$

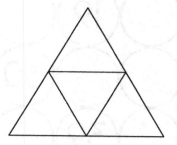

$$\frac{1}{4}$$

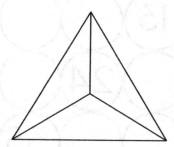

$$1$$

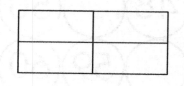

$$\frac{1}{4}$$

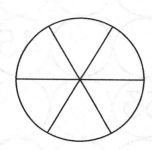

$$\frac{5}{6}$$

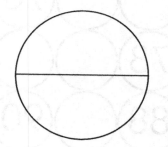

$$\frac{1}{2}$$

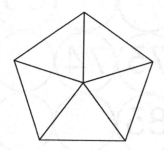

$$\frac{2}{5}$$

$$\frac{1}{5}$$

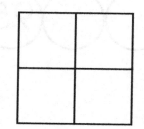

$$\frac{3}{4}$$

Solution on page 268

MISSING LETTERS

Complete the following words with the missing letters

Z V Y W T

_ak

_ip

_oy

_am

_oo

_in

_en

_et

_ax

_ea

_an

_ig

Solution on page 269

JOIN THE DOTS

Complete the dot-to-dot and color the hidden drawing

Write the name of the hidden animal

....

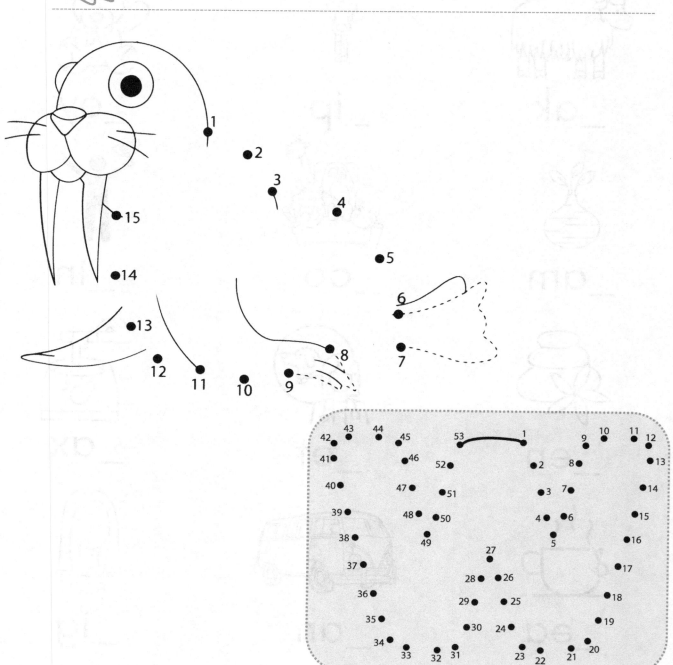

NAME THE WORD

Read the phrase, name the word that
describes the sentence, and say it out loud

1. This body part is used for listening.

2. This tells you the time.

3. This number comes after 10 and before 12.

4. This day comes after Wednesday and before Friday.

5. This season comes after winter.

6. This vehicle takes you over the water.

7. This appliance is used to heat food.

8. You use a ball and a racket to play this game.

Solution on page 270

WHISPER TO LOUD

Repeat the same sentence at different volumes, starting with a whisper and ending loudly

Lovely lady laughs

Lovely lady laughs

Lovely lady laughs

Lovely lady laughs

Lovely lady laughs

MAZE CHALLENGE

Find the correct path to connect the little birds

ODD ONE OUT

Look at the grid below. There is a shape that does not match. Circle it

i	i	i	i	!
i	i	i	i	i
i	i	i	i	i
i	i	i	i	i
i	i	i	i	i

Solution on page 271

TRUE OR FALSE

Read the sentences and circle true (T)
or false (F)

The Eiffel Tower is made entirely of iron. T / F

Dolphins are mammals. T / F

The human body has four lungs. T / F

Elephants are the only animals that can't
jump. T / F

Mount Everest is the tallest mountain in
the world. T / F

The capital of Italy is Paris. T / F

The sun is a planet. T / F

January is the first month of the year. T / F

Penguins can fly. T / F

Solution on page 272

WORD SEARCH - JOBS

Find the items listed below

```
A V M T I D O C T O R Q
M I E E A D O O K O R A
A E N A A D A A M S R A
F V C C C D O C T E R N
A W E H U T O H J C R U
R V D E A A O C T R N R
M V E R A N V R H E R S
E V N T A D I X T T R E
R V T T A D O C C A R A
A P I L O T O F T R R V
A V S U A D Z C G Y R E
A S T R O N A U T O H T
```

VET	FARMER	ASTRONAUT	TEACHER
PILOT	COACH	MECHANIC	DOCTOR
NURSE	ACTOR	SECRETARY	DENTIST

Solution on page 273

WORD LIST

Place the words below in the corresponding list

Water

Lion

Mouse

Cat

Madrid

Tea

Coke

Miami

Coffee

Bird

Venice

Wine

Chicago

London

Dog

Drinks

Cities

Animals

_____

_____

_____

_____

_____

_____

_____

_____

_____

_____

_____

_____

_____

_____

_____

Solution on page 274

FAVORITE FOODS

Think of 2 family members or friends. What are their favorite foods? Write them down

SCISSOR SKILLS

Color in the cat and cut along the lines

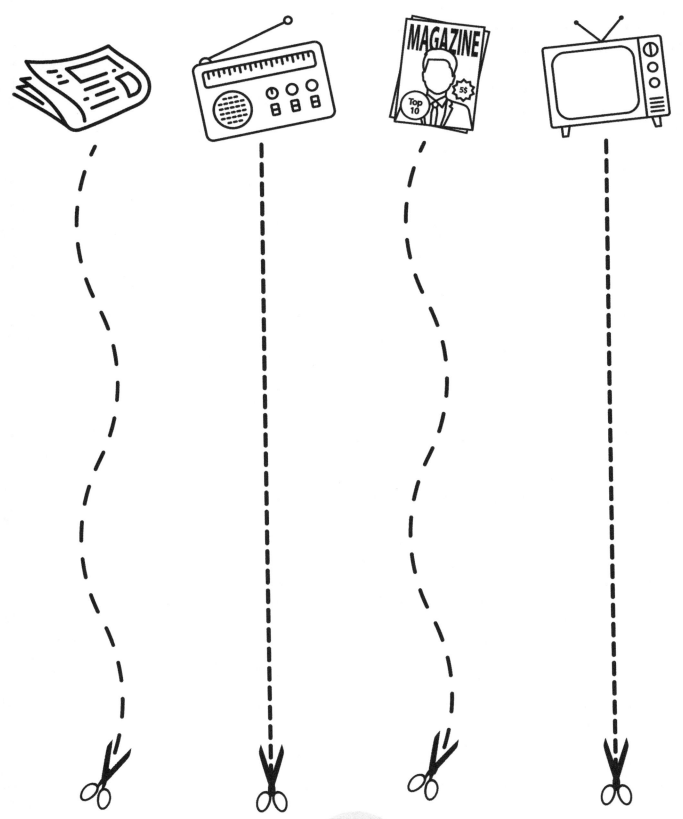

We left this page blank so as not to interfere with the previous exercise.

If you don't do the exercise, feel free to use this page to draw or write whatever you like!

TONGUE TWISTERS

Repeat each tongue twister 3 times,
starting slowly and gradually increasing
your speed

Toy boat, toy boat, toy boat.

A big black bear sat on a big black
rug.

Fresh fried fish, fish fresh fried, fried
fish fresh, fish fried fresh.

LETTER COMBINATIONS

Circle the 3 combinations that are
identical to the one in the rectangle

BVTO

BBVO	VTBO	LBVO	VLBO
BVVT	BTVO	BVTT	BVTT
BVTO	BVOT	PVOT	BVTO
OTBO	OVBT	LVVO	OTBV
BVLO	VTBO	RVOT	TOBV
BVTO	BVTU	PLBV	PVTO
TOOV	OTBV	PVBV	PVOB
TVBT	BVTO	OTBT	BVTB

Solution on page 275

DRAW THE EMOTION

Trace the word and draw the face of the emotion

Sleepy

WHAT TIME WAS IT 20 MIN AGO?

Look at the clocks, what time was it 20 minutes ago? Write it down

Solution on page 276

I PRACTICE OR I DON'T PRACTICE

Read these activities and categorize them based on whether you practice them or not

Reading

Stretching

Doing activity books

Being with my friends

Laughing

Dreaming

Going grocery shopping

Listening to music

Going to the movies

Swimming

I PRACTICE

I DON'T PRACTICE

COLOR THE LETTERS

Look at the word below and color the letters in it

 FANTASTIC

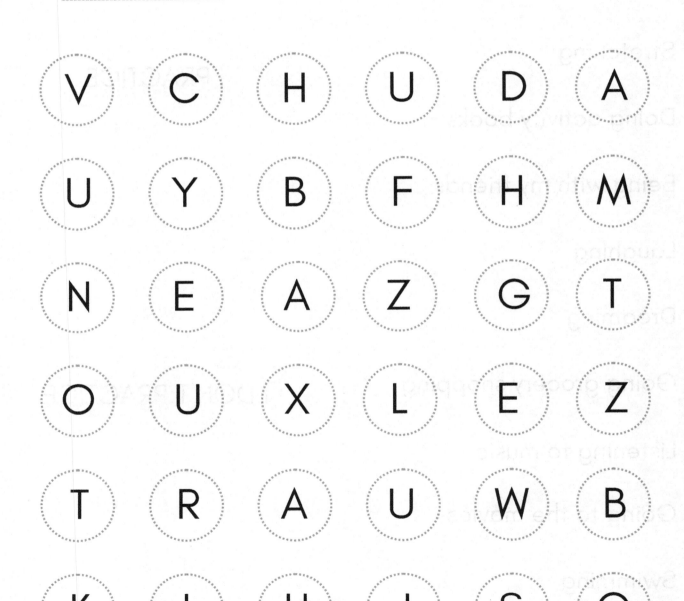

V	C	H	U	D	A
U	Y	B	F	H	M
N	E	A	Z	G	T
O	U	X	L	E	Z
T	R	A	U	W	B
K	I	H	J	S	Q

Solution on page 277

BODY POINTING

With your index finger, point to the part of the body indicated in each picture

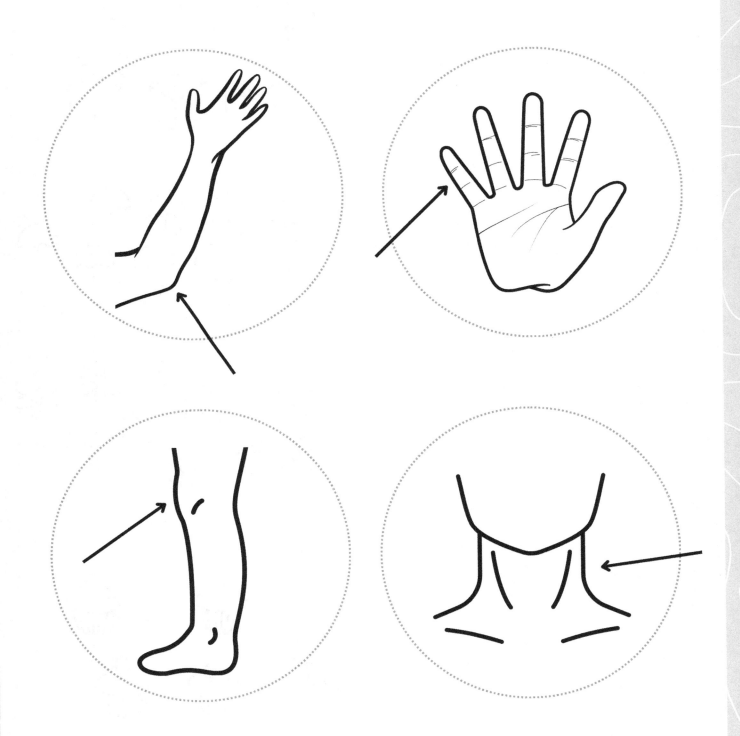

NUMBER OF OBJECTS

Trace and count the objects

6   Six

9   Nine

11   Eleven

5   Five

COLOR BY NUMBERS

Color the drawing with the color that corresponds to each number

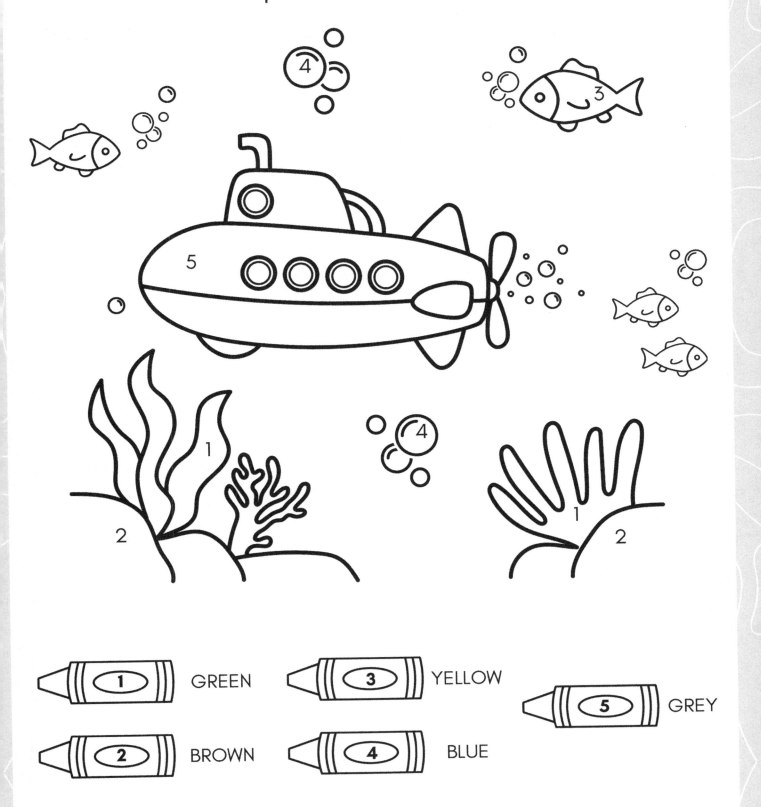

1 GREEN

3 YELLOW

5 GREY

2 BROWN

4 BLUE

We left this page blank so as not to interfere with the previous exercise.

If you don't do the exercise, feel free to use this page to draw or write whatever you like!

VISUAL SCANNING

Of the following objects, paint 5 of
them in color

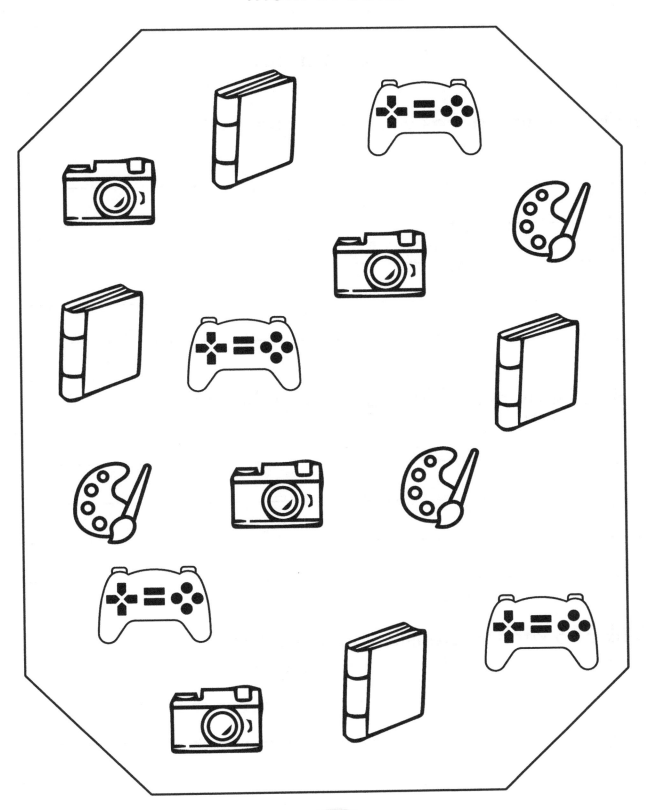

THOUGHT EXERCISE

Read the following sentences and write down whatever comes to mind

Household Items

Think of 5 appliances you use frequently:

1 _____

2 _____

3 _____

4 _____

5 _____

Think of 4 pieces of furniture in your home:

1 _____

2 _____

3 _____

4 _____

Think of 3 kitchen utensils you use often:

1 _____

2 _____

3 _____

YOUR OPINION MATTERS TO US

Now that you've finished the workbook, we truly hope this tool has been of great assistance to you.

At *Zanipe Books*, we are committed to consistently providing content that inspires as many people as possible to aid them in their recovery journey and to help them lead fulfilling, healthy lives, and your feedback is crucial in this endeavor.

If you found this book enjoyable, inspiring, and helpful, **please consider leaving a review on Amazon and sharing your thoughts with others by scanning the QR code provided.**

Your input can make a significant difference in helping others discover the valuable benefits of this book and in enabling us to continue improving.

Thank you so much for your support!

A GIFT FOR YOUR GRATITUDE

At Zanipe Books, we appreciate you choosing our book and trusting us.

As a token of our appreciation, we'd like to offer you a special gift: THE STROKE RECOVERY SUPPORT HANDBOOK.

This notebook facilitates communication between the individual and their family members or caregivers, acting as a companion and providing vital support throughout the recovery journey.

To claim your gift, **simply scan the QR code below and we will send you this notebook.** You can also email us at *info@zanipe.com* and include the magical word "*ZANIPERECOVERY*" in your email. We'll promptly respond with your gift.

If you have any questions, suggestions, or feedback about our book, just email us. We're here to help!

Thanks for your support!

Scan the QR Code to receive
THE STROKE RECOVERY SUPPORT HANDBOOK

Solutions

On the following pages, you can check if your answers to the exercises are correct or you can look at the solution for any exercise you're having trouble with.

If you would like to know the solution to any exercise and for any reason it is not included, you can email us at *info@zanipe.com* and we will send it to you.

COMPLETE THE PATTERN

Draw the shape that comes next in the pattern

FIND AND TRACE

Find and trace the numbers 1, 3, and 5

WHICH IS WHICH?

Connect the correct word to the
matching image

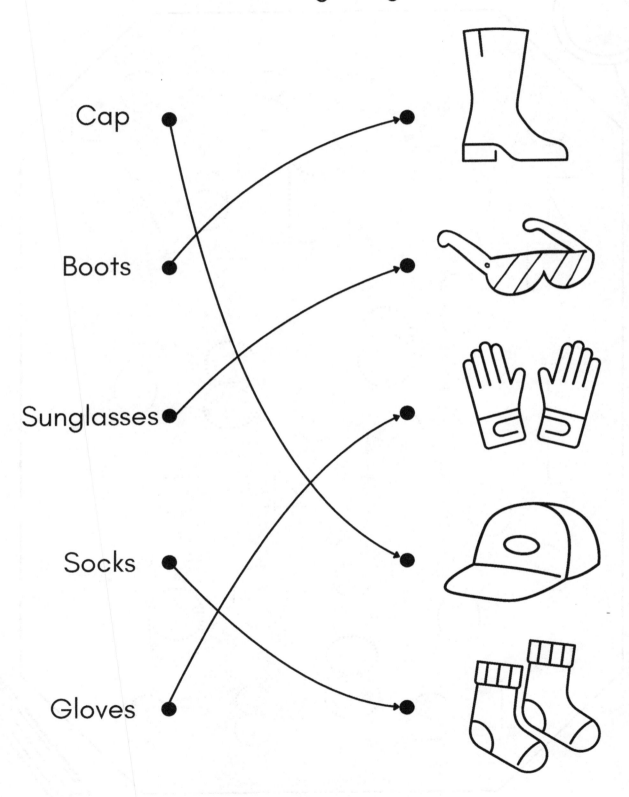

Cap

Boots

Sunglasses

Socks

Gloves

COUNT THE OBJECTS - WINTER

Count how many objects there are of
each and write them down

ice skate	2
boot	2
snowman	3
mug	3
mittens	6
jacket	2
scarf	1
snowflake	2
hat	3
fire	2

WHAT COMES NEXT?

Look at the sequence and identify which patterned block goes in the fourth spot, then mark it

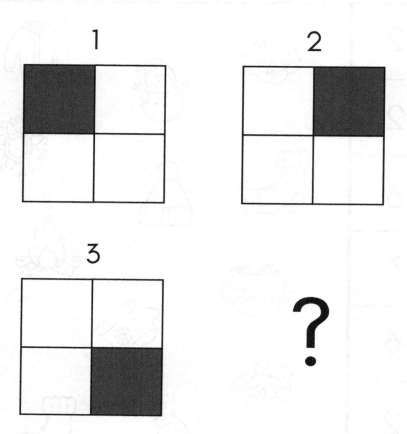

1

2

3

?

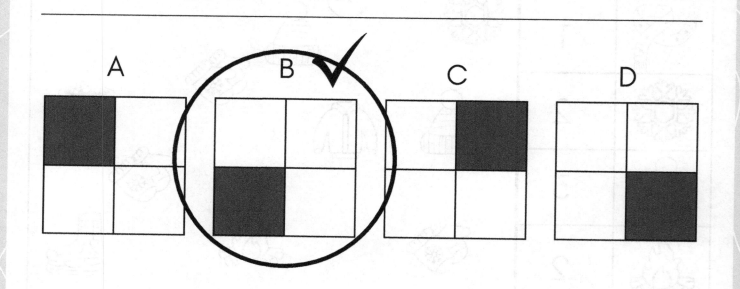

A   B ✓   C   D

WORD SEARCH - NUMBERS

Find the items listed below

```
R  S  G  T  W  E  L  V  E  I  T  A
B  H  E  E  M  I  O  K  P  V  A  S
D  X  E  V  A  S  I  X  O  O  L  D
E  O  H  L  E  T  C  C  E  N  A  T
L  T  N  C  O  N  E  I  T  E  D  H
E  I  I  C  T  W  E  M  O  T  K  R
V  R  N  S  E  A  F  I  V  E  S  E
E  C  E  H  N  V  A  A  V  G  F  E
N  U  W  V  E  C  F  E  C  R  L  A
B  O  T  W  O  L  K  O  O  T  U  M
B  V  T  E  P  L  C  H  U  E  P  N
E  E  I  G  H  T  I  R  E  R  F  R
```

ONE	FOUR	SEVEN	TEN
TWO	FIVE	EIGHT	ELEVEN
THREE	SIX	NINE	TWELVE

MISSING VOWELS

Complete the following words with the correct vowels.

 p_i_g

 d_o_g

 b_u_s

 b_e_d

 m_a_p

 b_a_g

 f_o_x

 b_u_g

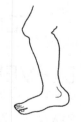 l_e_g

 r_a_t

COUNT THE OBJECTS - SPRING

Count how many objects there are of each and write them down

grass	3
rain cloud	3
potted plant	2
bee	4
umbrella	3
ladybug	5
butterfly	2
watering can	3
hose	1
flower	2

UNSCRAMBLE

Unscramble the letters to find the words

BREA	BEAR
ROHIN	RHINO
FORG	FROG
SANKE	SNAKE
GIRLLOA	GORILLA
EPHLENTA	ELEPHANT
CMAEL	CAMEL
CHTEEAH	CHEETAH
TCAUNO	TOUCAN
EGELA	EAGLE
FAMLIONG	FLAMINGO
CORDLIEOC	CROCODILE

204

CROSSWORD NUMBERS

Complete the crossword puzzle by filling in the blanks with the name of each number

MISSING LETTERS

Complete the following words with the missing letters

B   C   F   G   H

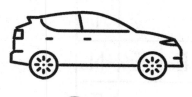

Car

Bat

Fan

Hut

Fly

Gum

Hen

Cut

Cat

Hot

Gas

Boy

206

UNSCRAMBLE

Unscramble the letters to find the words, then color the images

SORLFEW

FLOWERS

RBID

BIRD

BTUTEYRFL

BUTTERFLY

LUADYBG

LADYBUG

ETRE

TREE

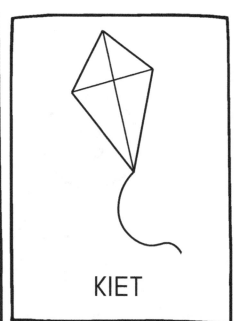

KIET

KIET

207

BUBBLE ADDITION

Add up these numbers and find the
answer in the bubbles

4 + 4 = _8_   4 + 3 = _7_

3 + 3 = _6_   4 + 5 = _9_

2 + 2 = _4_   1 + 2 = _3_

5 + 5 = _10_   2 + 3 = _5_

MISSING NUMBERS

Fill each heart with the missing numbers from 1 to 20

1 2 3 4

5 6 7 8

9 10 11 12

13 14 15 16

17 18 19 20

FRACTION EXERCISE

Circle the appropriate fraction from the provided options

$\frac{1}{2}$ $\frac{2}{3}$ $\frac{3}{4}$

$\frac{1}{3}$ $\frac{2}{4}$ $\frac{1}{4}$

$\frac{1}{3}$ $\frac{3}{5}$ $\frac{1}{2}$

$\frac{2}{3}$ $\frac{1}{5}$ $\frac{1}{2}$

WORD SEARCH - SPORTS

Find the items listed below

```
V  S  O  B  A  S  E  B  A  L  L  Q
G  O  L  F  A  D  U  A  C  O  A  S
S  O  L  U  M  D  G  S  B  T  S  W
C  Y  C  L  I  N  G  K  O  E  N  I
B  S  O  M  E  E  Y  E  L  N  E  M
H  O  C  K  E  Y  N  T  U  N  T  M
H  C  S  E  N  Y  B  B  N  I  B  I
U  C  T  E  N  D  I  A  A  S  O  N
T  E  J  N  O  S  T  L  L  O  A  G
F  R  U  G  B  Y  U  L  G  L  F  F
Y  F  D  D  T  S  L  T  G  P  S  D
S  F  O  O  T  B  A  L  L  L  O  H  T
```

JUDO	RUGBY	CYCLING
GOLF	FOOTBALL	SWIMMING
TENNIS	BASEBALL	VOLLEYBALL
SOCCER	HOCKEY	BASKETBALL

TRUE OR FALSE

Read the sentences and circle true (T) or false (F)

Trees are blue. T / F

Trees have brown trunks and green leaves.

Grass is green. T / F

Trees have branches. T / F

Grass has petals. T / F

The grass doesn't have petals, the petals are on the flowers.

Birds are mammals. T / F

Birds are animals but not mammals.

There are 365 days in a year. T / F

Cats can speak English. T / F

Cats do not talk, cats meow.

Each season lasts four months. T / F

Chickens lay eggs. T / F

WHAT TIME IS IT?

Look at the clocks, what time is it?
Write it down

3 : 30

1 : 30

8 : 30

9 : 30

11 : 30

11 : 00

4 : 30

6 : 30

5 : 30

SHOWING EMOTION

Match the following images with the emotions they best capture. Then try showing the same emotion yourself

Love   Surprise

Anger   Boredom

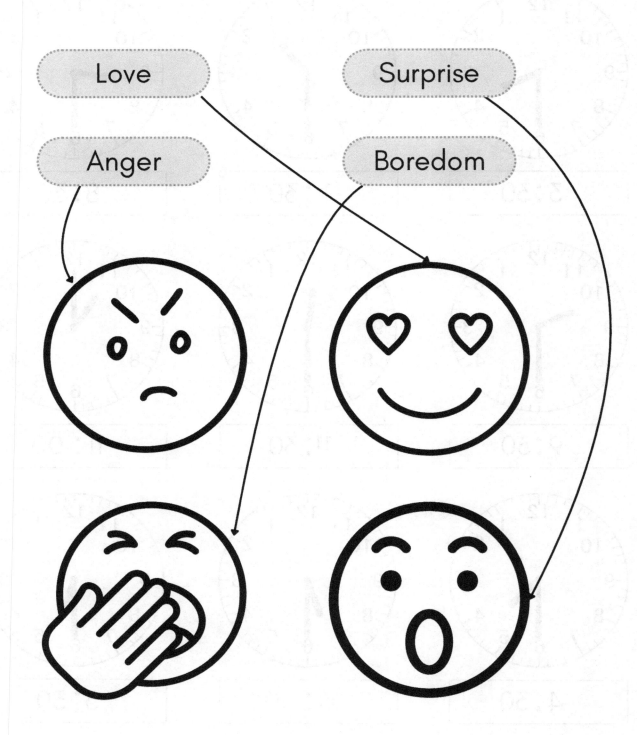

WORD LIST

Place the words below in the corresponding list

Burger

Sandwich

Tango

Flamenco

Fencing

Swimming

Tennis

Tacos

Pizza

Basketball

Mambo

Soccer

Spaghetti

Reggaeton

Samba

Dances	Sports	Food
Reggaeton	Swimming	Sandwich
Tango	Basketball	Burger
Mambo	Fencing	Pizza
Samba	Tennis	Spaghetti
Flamenco	Soccer	Tacos

COLOR THE LETTERS

Look at the word below and color the letters in it

🔍 COLORFUL

V	C	H	U	D	A
U	Y	B	F	H	M
N	E	A	Z	G	P
O	U	X	L	E	O
T	R	A	U	W	B
K	I	H	J	L	Q

WRITTEN TIME

Draw a line to match each time to each written time

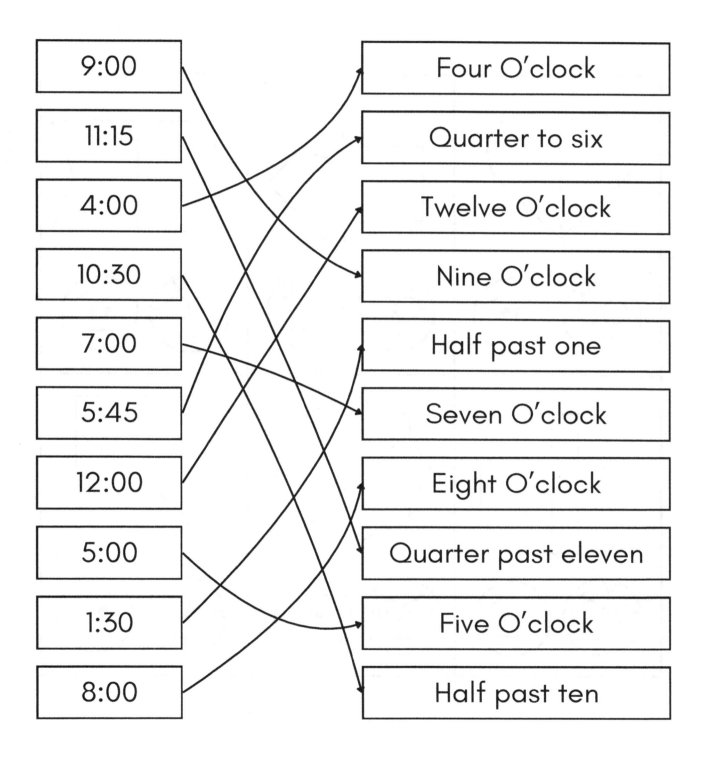

9:00	Four O'clock
11:15	Quarter to six
4:00	Twelve O'clock
10:30	Nine O'clock
7:00	Half past one
5:45	Seven O'clock
12:00	Eight O'clock
5:00	Quarter past eleven
1:30	Five O'clock
8:00	Half past ten

HALF OR NOT?

Color the happy face for shapes that are halves. Color the sad face for shapes that are not halves

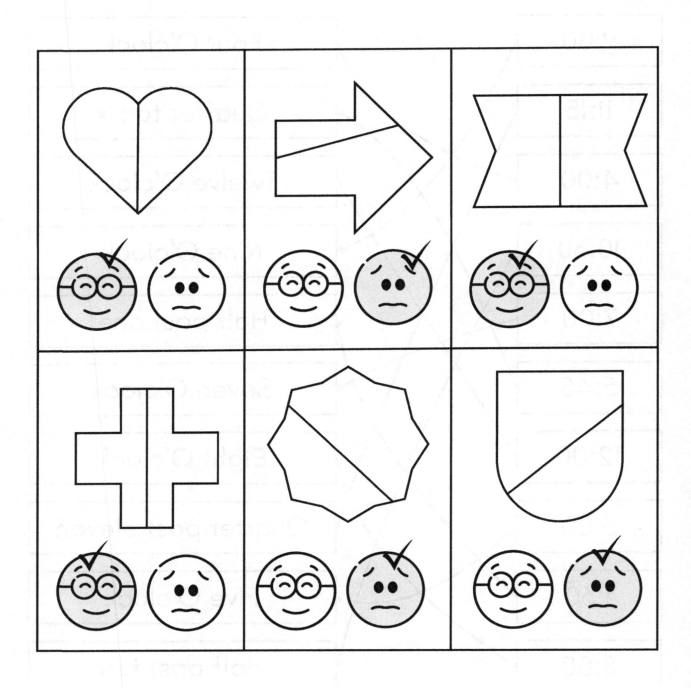

FIND AND TRACE

Find and trace the letters A, B, and C

WHAT'S THE WEATHER LIKE?

Connect the correct weather word to the matching image

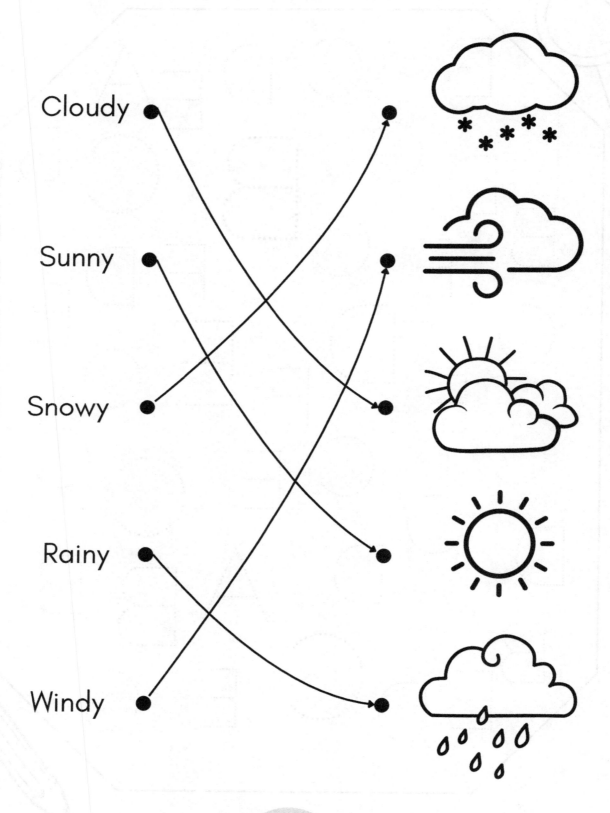

Cloudy

Sunny

Snowy

Rainy

Windy

CROSSWORD - VEGETABLES

Complete the crossword using the
given clues

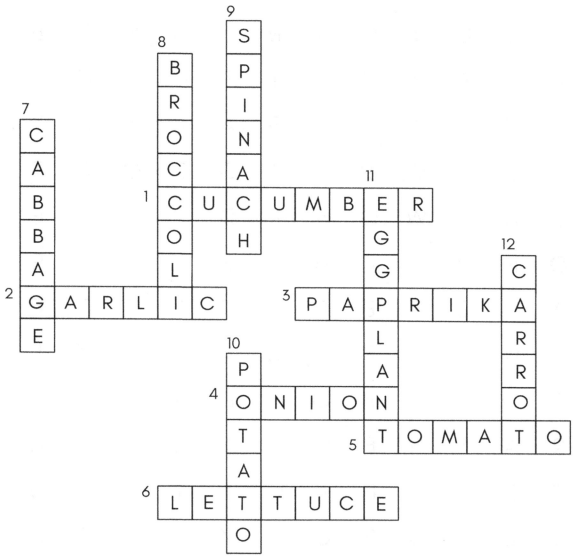

Across

1. _____

2. _____

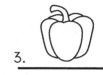

3. _____

4. _____

5. _____

6. _____

Down

7. _____

8. _____

9. _____

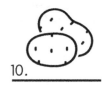

10. _____

11. _____

12. _____

WORD SEARCH - SPRING

Find the items listed below

```
R  E  D  Y  C  N  E  B  U  N  D  B
A  P  A  A  S  E  I  L  M  P  U  U
I  K  I  T  E  S  S  A  B  I  A  T
N  J  S  C  P  T  I  D  R  C  P  T
C  A  Y  W  G  A  R  D  E  N  A  E
O  N  N  L  P  N  N  F  L  I  R  R
A  U  G  S  E  E  B  T  L  C  T  F
T  U  L  I  P  A  B  A  A  N  Y  L
I  O  S  U  H  O  L  D  A  I  S  Y
R  A  I  N  B  O  O  T  S  H  I  H
G  F  I  C  H  A  O  I  T  Y  A  U
B  L  O  S  S  O  M  Y  B  U  G  G
```

KITE	NEST	DAISY	TULIP
GARDEN	RAINCOAT	BLOOM	PICNIC
UMBRELLA	RAINBOOTS	BLOSSOM	BUTTERFLY

UNSCRAMBLE

Unscramble the letters to find the
words, then color the images

SOOBT

BOOTS

WNOS

SNOW

OHCCTLAOE

CHOCOLATE

THA

HAT

ISKS

SKIS

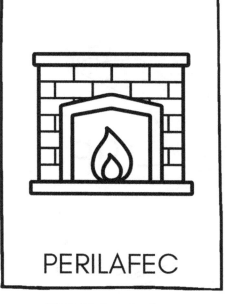

PERILAFEC

FIREPLACE

MISSING LETTERS

Complete the following words with the missing letters

P T S W

<u>S</u>tar

<u>P</u>lum

<u>S</u>kip

<u>T</u>ram

<u>S</u>top

<u>S</u>wim

<u>W</u>rap

<u>S</u>now

<u>P</u>ray

<u>S</u>wan

<u>T</u>able

<u>S</u>hop

COUNT THE OBJECTS - EASTER

Count how many objects there are of
each and write them down

(flower)	4
(egg)	1
(candy)	3
(book)	4
(chick)	1
(bunny)	3
(chick in egg)	2
(egg with flower)	1
(carrot)	4
(tulip)	2

FRIENDS OF NUMBER 20

Complete the following problems to
show the number 20

$12 + \boxed{8} = 20$ $14 + \boxed{6} = 20$

$\boxed{16} + 4 = 20$ $\boxed{15} + 5 = 20$

$10 + \boxed{10} = 20$ $6 + \boxed{14} = 20$

$\boxed{7} + 13 = 20$ $\boxed{11} + 9 = 20$

$7 + \boxed{13} = 20$ $3 + \boxed{17} = 20$

$\boxed{5} + 15 = 20$ $\boxed{9} + 11 = 20$

SUM THE DICE

Fill the right number box with the number on the dice

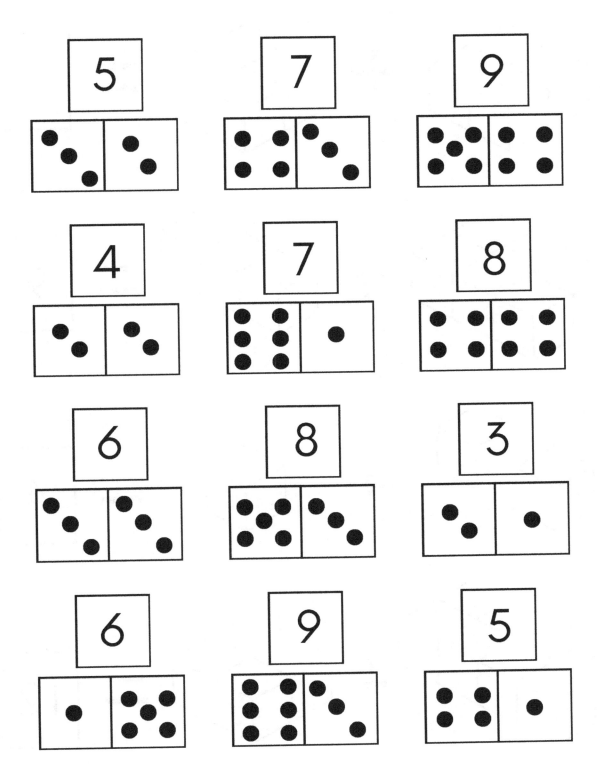

FIND THE SUM

Count the cubes and write the sum in the box

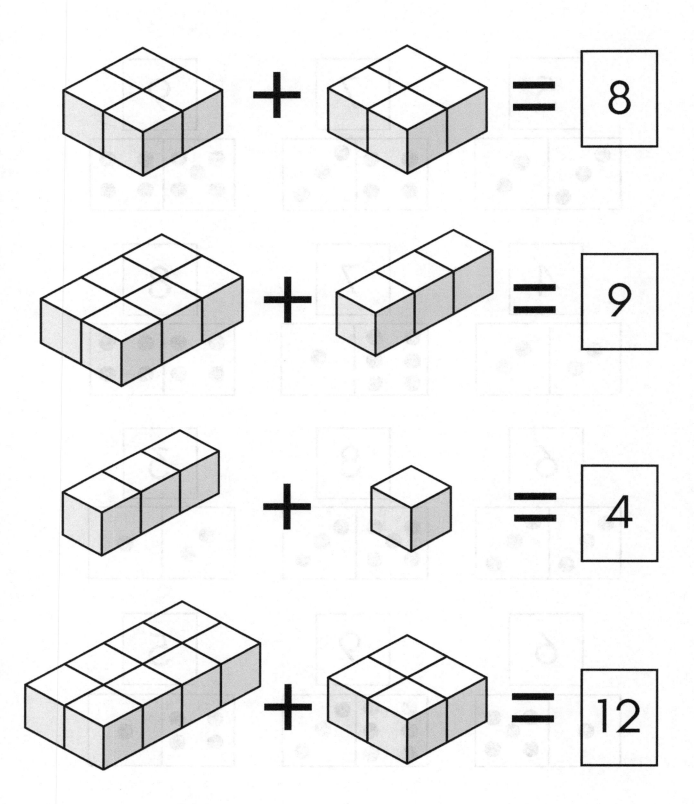

ODD MAN OUT

Below are lists of different topics.
Circle the word that does not belong
to the group

SEPTEMBER

APRIL

(BOOTS)

MAY

WALL

WINDOW

(SOCKS)

FLOOR

COFFEE

WATER

(ORANGES)

TEA

BASKETBALL

SOCCER

(SANDALS)

SURFING

SISTER

MOTHER

(SHAMPOO)

FATHER

LONDON

PARIS

(BEACH)

ISTANBUL

DRAW THE HANDS ON THE CLOCK TO SHOW THE TIME

Seven o'clock

Four o'clock

Ten o'clock

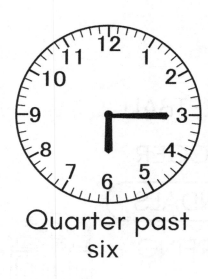

Quarter past six

Quarter past eleven

Quarter past two

Half past nine

Half past six

Half past three

WHAT JOB IS IT?

Assign the activities listed below to the correct person

Taxi Driver (T)   Chef (C)   Architect (A)

___Chef___ Setting up menus

__Architect__ Visits buildings under construction

Taxi Driver Makes car rides more comfortable

Taxi Driver Accompanies people to their homes

___Chef___ Tasting dishes before serving

Taxi Driver Works in a car

___Chef___ Always thinking of new recipes

__Architect__ Works on projects

__Architect__ Constructs buildings

Taxi Driver Charges by the minute

__Architect__ Has a good sense of aesthetic

___Chef___ Prepping the kitchen before meal times

Taxi Driver Works sitting down

__Architect__ Designs building plans

___Chef___ Overseeing kitchen staff

WORD SEARCH - FARM ANIMALS

Find the items listed below

```
R A G E S R A B B I T A
B H I O M I O K P V A S
D X E R A S A C O W L D
U O H L A T C C E R A O
C T O C O M E I T I D N
K I R C H W E M O T K K
N R S S E A L G O O S E
R C E H N V A A V G F Y
E U W V E C H I C K L E
P I G K T L K C O T U M
B V T E P L S H E E P N
E D O V E T I R E L F R
```

RABBIT	SHEEP	PIG	CHICK
DONKEY	GOAT	COW	DOVE
GOOSE	DUCK	HEN	HORSE

MATCH THE HOMOPHONES

Highlight the word that names each picture

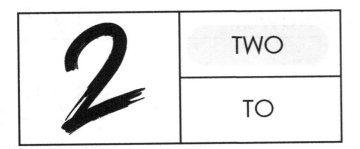

TWO

TO

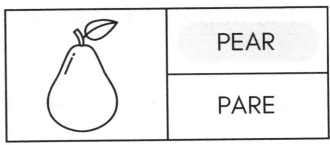

PEAR

PARE

FLOWER

FLOUR

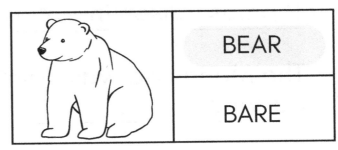

BEAR

BARE

CELL

SELL

KNIGHT

NIGHT

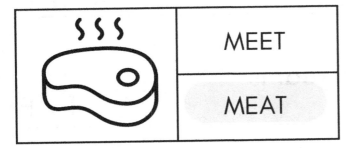

MEET

MEAT

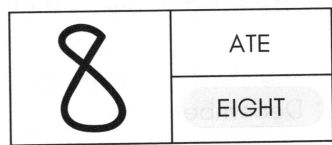

ATE

EIGHT

TRUE OR FALSE

Read the sentences and circle true (T)
or false (F)

The capital of Canada is Ottawa.   T / F

Octopuses have eight legs.   T / F

Thomas Edison invented the light bulb.   T / F

The Mona Lisa was painted by Leonardo
da Vinci.   T / F

The Statue of Liberty was a gift from
France to the United States.   T / F

A triangle has three sides.   T / F

Watermelon grows on trees.   T / F
Watermelon grows on vines on the ground.

The shortest month of the year is
December.   T / F
The shortest month of the year is February.

ODD ONE OUT

Look at the grid below. There is a
shape that does not match. Circle it

A	A	A	A	A
A	A	A	A	A
A	A	A	4	A
A	A	A	A	A
A	A	A	A	A

LETTER COMBINATIONS

Circle the 3 combinations that are
identical to the one in the rectangle

ALNM

NLMA	NAML	ANML	LANM
LNAM	LAMN	NMAL	AMLN
ANLM	**ALNM**	LMNA	NLAM
MLNA	BNMA	MALN	LNMA
ALNM	MANB	**ALNM**	BNMA
MANL	AMNL	NMLA	LBMA
MNLA	MNBH	MNAL	BLNM
MLAN	BANM	ALMN	MBLN

WHICH IS WHICH ON THANKSGIVING?

Connect the correct word to the matching image

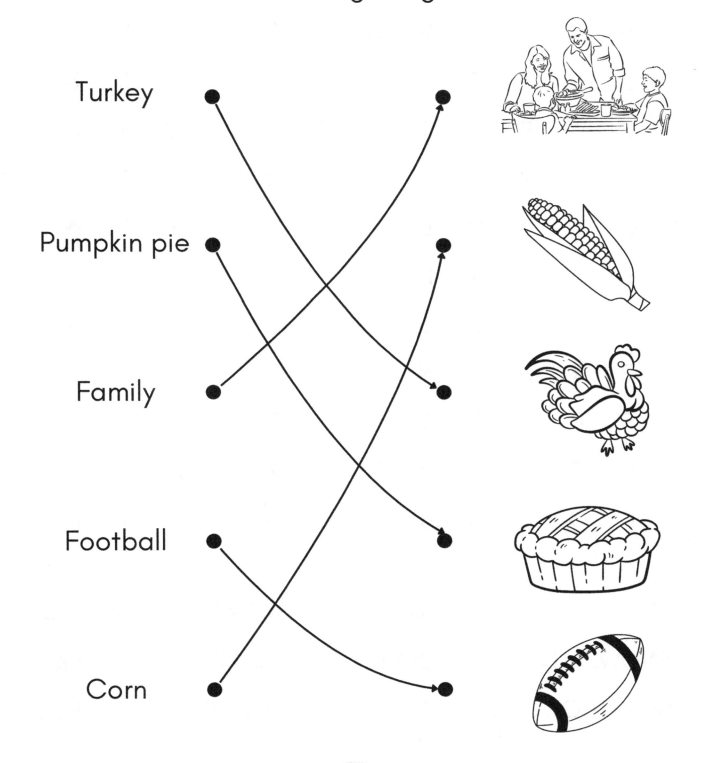

Turkey

Pumpkin pie

Family

Football

Corn

WORD SEARCH - WINTER

Find the items listed below

```
C S N O W C S O C O L D
H N L P M H C O L T U U
J O I C I U A O F I R S
S W E A T E R O L C I N
N B Y M T S F N A D C O
G A J U E F O C K I K W
L L B M N T T E E S O M
E L D B S K I I N G T A
R R P R N S E C T S E N
F R E E Z E C T O R I S
D F C O N F O V L A K N
H O T C H O C O L A T E
```

SNOWMAN   SNOW   SWEATER   SKIING

SNOWBALL   COLD   SCARF   FLAKE

HOT CHOCOLATE   COAT   MITTENS   FREEZE

UNSCRAMBLE

Unscramble the letters to find the
words, then color the images

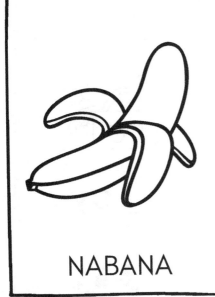

NABANA

BANANA

PPLEA

APPLE

APERG

GRAPE

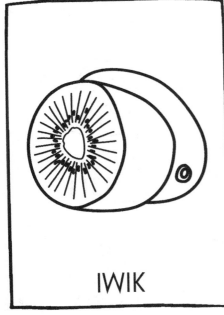

IWIK

KIWI

ERRWABTRSY

STRAWBERRY

REAP

PEAR

MISSING LETTERS

Complete the following words with the missing letters

M N D P T S

Nut

Sad

Toy

Tap

Mop

Dad

Pot

Mum

Nun

Sit

Pin

Dig

CROSSWORD - CLOTHES

Complete the crossword using the
given clues

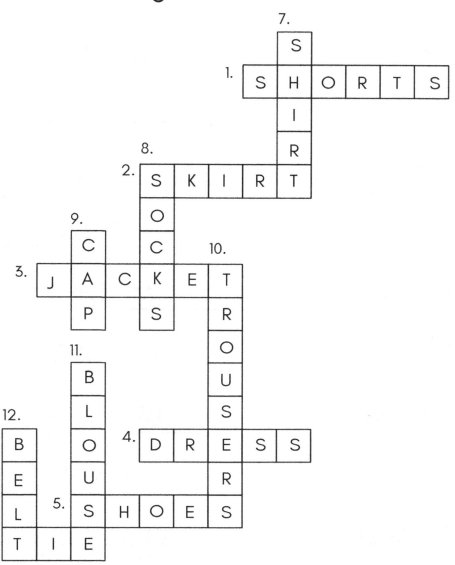

Across

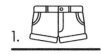 1. _____

 2. _____

 3. _____

 4. _____

 5. _____

 6. _____

Down

 7. _____

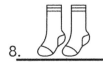 8. _____

 9. _____

 10. _____

 11. _____

 12. _____

UNSCRAMBLE

Unscramble the letters to find the words

ANTU   AUNT

SNO   SON

UCLEN   UNCLE

SESTIR   SISTER

METHOR   MOTHER

FRETHA   FATHER

BOERTHR   BROTHER

GARNDAP   GRANDPA

GRMANDA   GRANDMA

SBLINISG   SIBLINGS

CUONISS   COUSINS

DUAGHRET   DAUGHTER

COUNT THE OBJECTS - HALLOWEEN

Count how many objects there are of
each and write them down

broom	2
bat	3
ghost	3
gravestone	1
bone	4
hat	6
skull	1
cauldron	2
pumpkin	1
spider	2

DECOMPOSITION

Break these numbers down into tens
and units

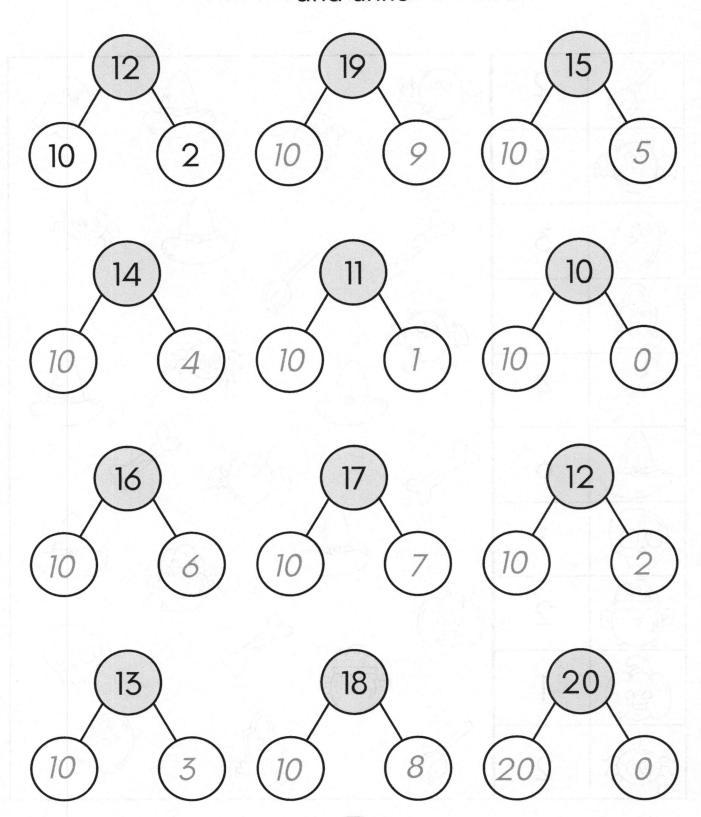

MATCHING ADDITION

Add up these numbers and match the result with the numbers on the right

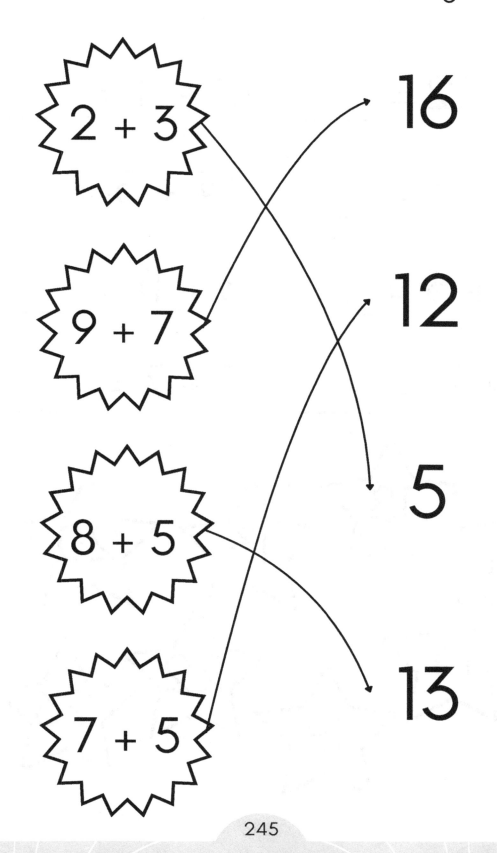

2 + 3

9 + 7

8 + 5

7 + 5

16

12

5

13

STARS ADDITION

Add up these numbers and find the answer in the stars

10 + 12 = _22_　　19 + 4 = _13_

9 + 9 = _18_　　24 + 3 = _27_

21 + 5 = _26_　　8 + 11 = _19_

9 + 11 = _20_　　7 + 7 = _14_

SUM THE DICE

Fill the right number box with the number on the dice

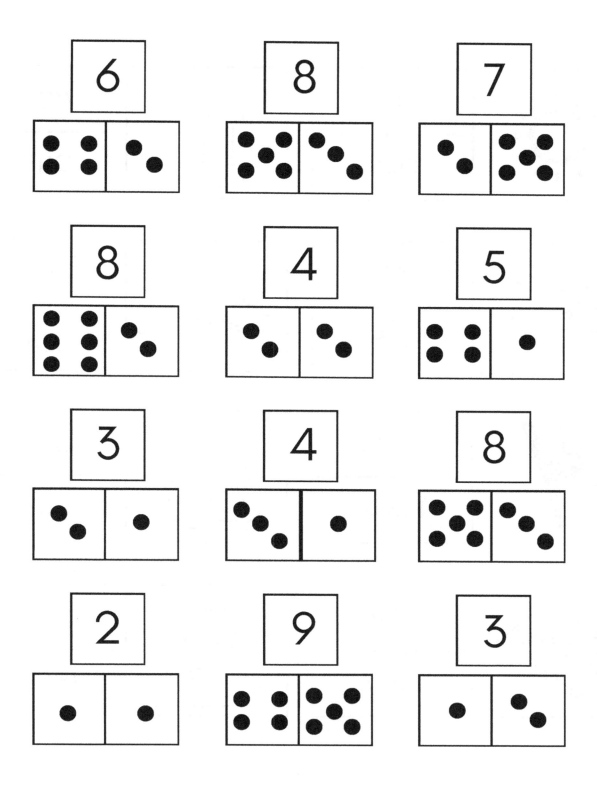

MATCH THE HOMOPHONES

Highlight the word that names each picture

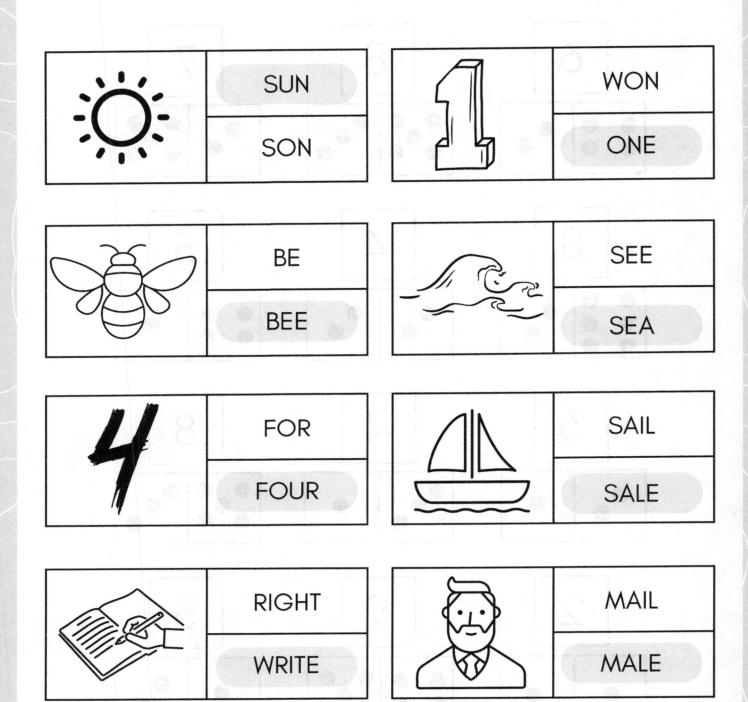

SUN	
SON	

WON	
ONE	

BE	
BEE	

SEE	
SEA	

FOR	
FOUR	

SAIL	
SALE	

RIGHT	
WRITE	

MAIL	
MALE	

WHAT JOB IS IT?

Assign the activities listed below to the correct person

| Doctor (D) | Teacher (T) | Firefighter (F) |

___Teacher___ Grading tests

___Firefighter___ Risks their life working

___Firefighter___ Puts out fires

___Doctor___ Works in a white coat

___Doctor___ Cares for patients

___Firefighter___ Wears heavy gear for work

___Teacher___ Preparing lesson materials

___Firefighter___ Wears a helmet on a daily basis

___Doctor___ Prescribes medication for patients

___Firefighter___ Needs to be in good shape

___Teacher___ Assigning homework

___Teacher___ Measuring students' progress

___Doctor___ Visits patients

___Teacher___ Explaining the lesson

___Doctor___ Has studied the human body

SHADOW MATCHING

Draw a line from each item to its matching shadow

250

ODD ONE OUT

Look at the grid below. There is a shape that does not match. Circle it

7	7	7	7	7
7	7	7	7	7
7	7	7	7	7
T	7	7	7	7
7	7	7	7	7

ODD MAN OUT

Below are lists of different pieces of clothing. Circle the word that does not belong to the group

HAT

BOOTS

SHOES

SLIPPERS

BAG

SUIT

DRESS

BLOUSE

COAT

T-SHIRT

JACKET

SWEATER

JACKET

BLOUSE

JEANS

SHIRT

EARRINGS

NECKLACE

BRACELET

BAG

PANTS

SHIRT

WATCH

PAJAMAS

TRUE OR FALSE

Read the sentences and circle true (T)
or false (F)

There are eleven months in a year. T / **F**

No, there are 12 months in a year.

Penguins can fly. T / **F**

Penguins are non-flying birds.

November is the last month of the year. T / **F**

The last month of the year is December.

Giraffes have short necks. T / **F**

Giraffes have long necks.

The sun is smaller than a soccer ball. T / **F**

The sun is much larger than a soccer ball.

Apples are a type of fruit. **T** / F

There are stars in the sky. **T** / F

Ice cream is typically served hot. T / **F**

Ice cream is typically served cold.

DRAW THE HANDS ON THE CLOCK TO SHOW THE TIME

Two o'clock

Half past five

Quarter past one

Seven o'clock

Quarter past eight

Ten o'clock

Half past eleven

Nine o'clock

Quarter to six

COLOR THE LETTERS

Look at the word below and color the letters in it

 MANDALA

V C H U D A

U Y B F H M

N E A Z G P

O U X L E Z

T R A U W B

K I H J S Q

WHICH IS WHICH ON CHRISTMAS?

Connect the correct word to the matching image

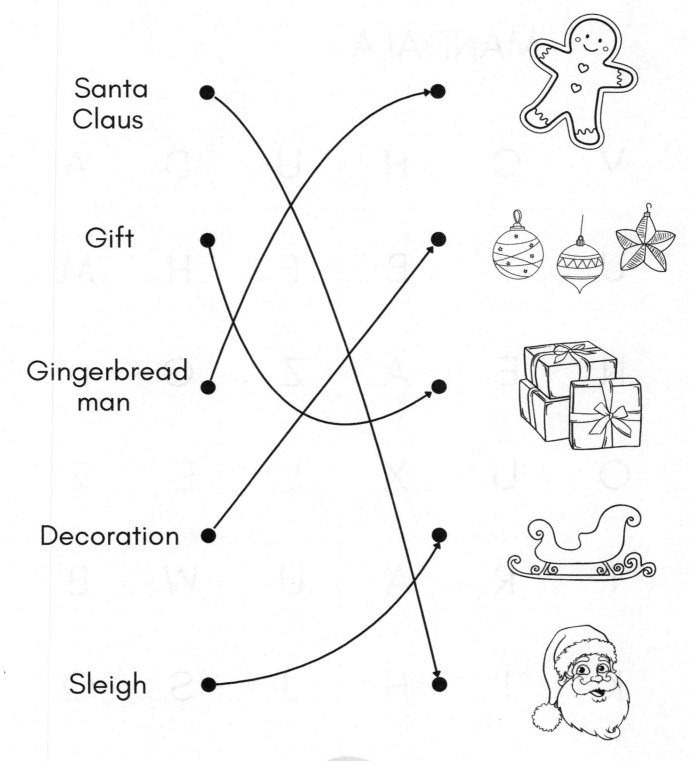

Santa Claus

Gift

Gingerbread man

Decoration

Sleigh

WHAT COMES NEXT?

Look at the sequence and identify which patterned block goes in the fourth spot, then mark it

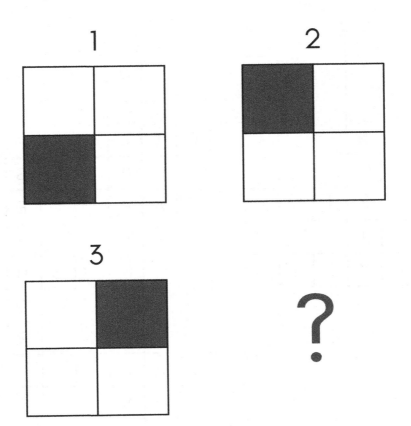

1   2

3   ?

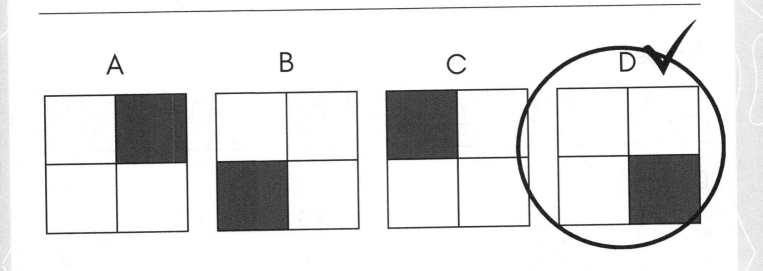

A   B   C   D ✓

CROSSWORD - SEA ANIMALS

Complete the crossword using the given clues

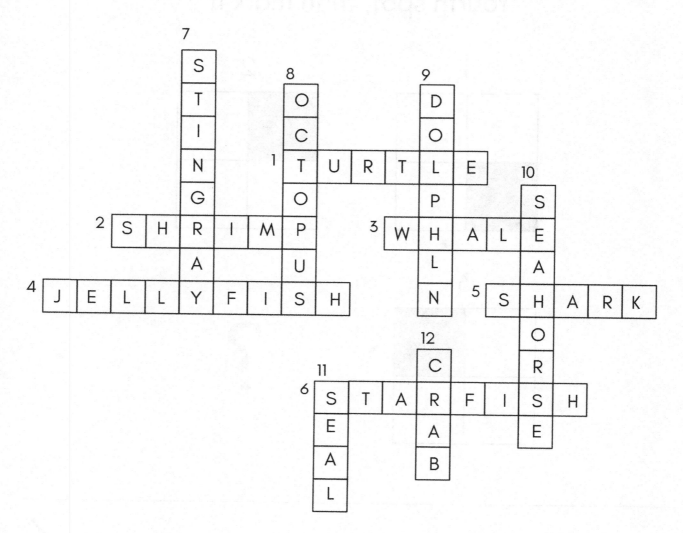

Across

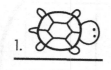 1.

 2.

 3.

 4.

 5.

 6.

Down

 7.

 8.

 9.

 10.

 11.

 12.

WORD SEARCH - FAMILY MEMBERS

Find the items listed below

```
S Y F A T H E R T R T U R Q
M O E E A D O A U N T A
S R N C M D A A N C R G
F P C C O D O C L R R
G T A B T U O H L E N A
R H D R H I S T E R N N
A E E O E N V I S E N D
N R N T R N I X N T R M
D V T H A D T C C H R A
P P I E O S I S T E R V
A V S R A D Z C G R R E
S D A U G H T E R O H T
```

SON   FATHER   COUSIN   GRANDPA

AUNT   MOTHER   BROTHER   GRANDMA

UNCLE   SISTER   PARENTS   DAUGHTER

MISSING LETTERS

Complete the following words with the missing letters

B C F G H

Fish   **B**ird   **F**arm

Corn   **H**and   **G**ift

Camp   **G**olf   **H**arp

Half   **F**ork   **B**unk

UNSCRAMBLE

Unscramble the letters to find the words, then color the images. Hint! Look at the monument, in which city is it located?

ONABLCEAR

BARCELONA

SAPRI

PARIS

OARM

ROMA

WNE ROYK

NEW YORK

NOODNL

LONDON

RIEVIRA AYMA

RIVIERA MAYA

SHADOW MATCHING

Draw a line from each item to its
matching shadow

COUNT THE OBJECTS - CHRISTMAS

Count how many objects there are of
each and write them down

Object	Count
🎄	3
🎗	3
💡	1
🧑	5
🍬	2
🍀	1
🎁	2
⚪	1
🎅	3
🧦	2

FRIENDS OF NUMBER 10

Complete the following problems to show the number 10

$8 + \boxed{2} = 10$ $0 + \boxed{10} = 10$

$\boxed{4} + 6 = 10$ $\boxed{1} + 9 = 10$

$2 + \boxed{8} = 10$ $7 + \boxed{3} = 10$

$\boxed{6} + 4 = 10$ $\boxed{5} + 5 = 10$

$10 + \boxed{0} = 10$ $3 + \boxed{7} = 10$

$\boxed{5} + 5 = 10$ $\boxed{9} + 1 = 10$

STARS ADDITION

Add up these numbers and find the answer in the stars

31 + 2 = _33_   10 + 5 = _15_

20 + 5 = _25_   9 + 2 = _11_

19 + 7 = _26_   7 + 10 = _17_

17 + 3 = _20_   13 + 3 = _16_

MISSING NUMBERS

Fill each shape with the missing numbers from 31 to 50

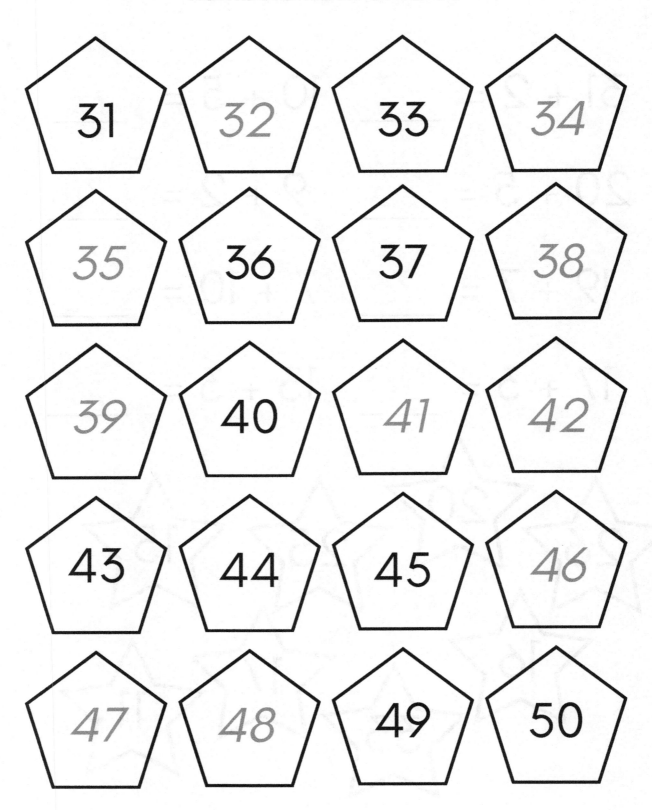

COUNT TO 100

Fill in the missing numbers and
count to 100

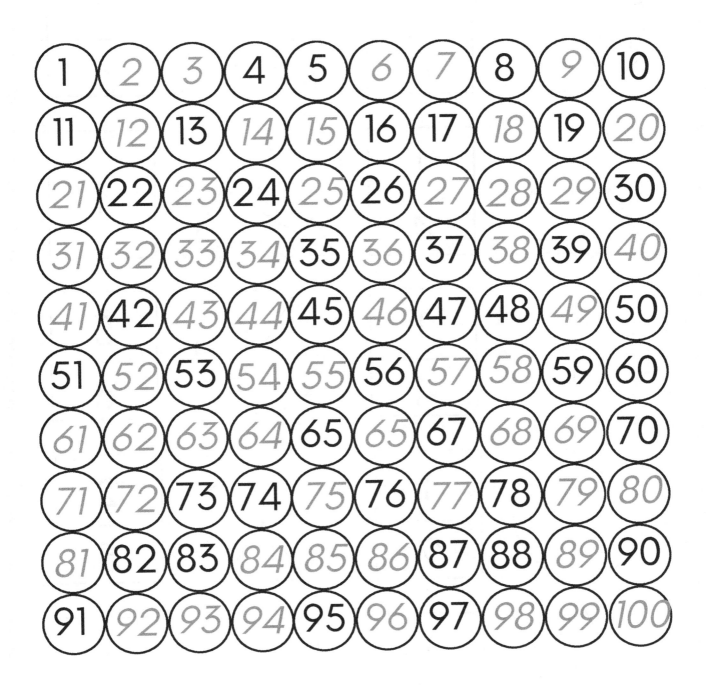

COLOR THE PORTIONS

Color the portions to represent the fraction

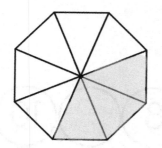 $\dfrac{3}{8}$ 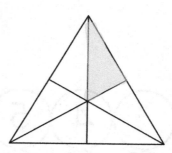 $\dfrac{1}{6}$

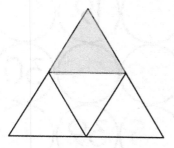 $\dfrac{1}{4}$ 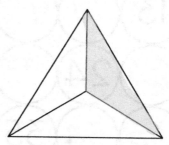 1

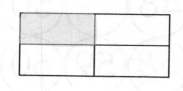 $\dfrac{1}{4}$ 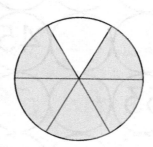 $\dfrac{5}{6}$

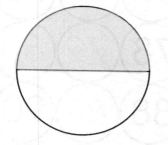 $\dfrac{1}{2}$ 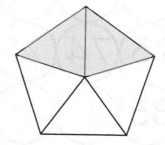 $\dfrac{2}{5}$

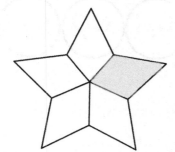 $\dfrac{1}{5}$ 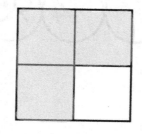 $\dfrac{3}{4}$

MISSING LETTERS

Complete the following words with the missing letters

Z V Y W T

Yak

Zip

Toy

Yam

Zoo

Win

Zen

Vet

Wax

Tea

Van

Wig

NAME THE WORD

Read the phrase, name the word that describes the sentence, and say it out loud

1. This body part is used for listening.
   Ears

2. This tells you the time.
   Watch

3. This number comes after 10 and before 12.
   Eleven

4. This day comes after Wednesday and before Friday.
   Thursday

5. This season comes after winter.
   Spring

6. This vehicle takes you over the water.
   Boat

7. This appliance is used to heat food.
   Microwave

8. You use a ball and a racket to play this game.
   Tennis

ODD ONE OUT

Look at the grid below. There is a shape that does not match. Circle it

i	i	i	i	!
i	i	i	i	i
i	i	i	i	i
i	i	i	i	i
i	i	i	i	i

TRUE OR FALSE

Read the sentences and circle true (T) or false (F)

The Eiffel Tower is made entirely of iron.   T / F

Dolphins are mammals.   T / F

The human body has four lungs.   T / F
The human body has only two lungs.

Elephants are the only animals that can't jump.   T / F
There are other animals that also cannot jump.

Mount Everest is the tallest mountain in the world.   T / F

The capital of Italy is Paris   T / F
No, the capital of Italy is Rome

The sun is a planet.   T / F
No, the sun is a star.

January is the first month of the year.   T / F

WORD SEARCH - JOBS

Find the items listed below

```
A  V  M  T  I  D  O  C  T  O  R  Q
M  I  E  E  A  D  O  O  K  O  R  A
A  E  N  A  A  D  A  A  M  S  R  A
F  V  C  C  C  D  O  C  T  E  R  N
A  W  E  H  U  T  O  H  J  C  R  U
R  V  D  E  A  A  O  C  T  R  N  R
M  V  E  R  A  N  V  R  H  E  R  S
E  V  N  T  A  D  I  X  T  T  R  E
R  V  T  T  A  D  O  C  C  A  R  A
A  P  I  L  O  T  O  F  T  R  R  V
A  V  S  U  A  D  Z  C  G  Y  R  E
A  S  T  R  O  N  A  U  T  O  H  T
```

VET	FARMER	ASTRONAUT	TEACHER
PILOT	COACH	MECHANIC	DOCTOR
NURSE	ACTOR	SECRETARY	DENTIST

WORD LIST

Place the words below in the corresponding list

Water

Lion

Mouse

Madrid

Coke

Tea

Cat

Coffee

Venice

Bird

Miami

Chicago

Dog

London

Wine

Drinks	Cities	Animals
Water	Madrid	Lion
Coke	Chicago	Dog
Coffee	Venice	Bird
Tea	London	Cat
Wine	Miami	Mouse

LETTER COMBINATIONS

Circle the 4 combinations that are
identical to the one in the rectangle

BVTO

BBVO	VTBO	LBVO	VLBO
BVVT	BTVO	BVTT	BVTT
(BVTO)	BVOT	PVOT	(BVTO)
OTBO	OVBT	LVVO	OTBV
BVLO	VTBO	RVOT	TOBV
(BVTO)	BVTU	PLBV	PVTO
TOOV	OTBV	PVBV	PVOB
TVBT	(BVTO)	OTBT	BVTB

WHAT TIME WAS IT 20 MIN AGO?

Look at the clocks, what time was it 20 minutes ago? Write it down

3 :00

6 :40

3 :40

8 :40

11:00

3 :20

5 :40

8 : 20

12 : 40

COLOR THE LETTERS

Look at the word below and color the letters in it

 FANTASTIC

V	C	H	U	D	A
U	Y	B	F	H	M
N	E	A	Z	G	T
O	U	X	L	E	Z
T	R	A	U	W	B
K	I	H	J	S	Q

Made in the USA
Monee, IL
20 October 2024

68367331R10155